SPARK OF THE DIVINE

RAJINDER SINGH

PRAISE FOR SANT RAJINDER SINGH'S BOOKS

"Sant Rajinder Singh Ji explains how peace can be created through meditation and inner reflection. There will be no lasting peace unless individual human beings have some sense of inner peace. To create inner peace it is necessary to calm the mind, hence the importance of meditation. I greatly appreciate Sant Rajinder Singh Ji's contribution here to the goal of peace that we are all working towards. May readers of this book find peace within themselves through meditation and so foster a greater sense of peace throughout the world."

– H.H. the Dalai Lama

"This outstanding handbook reflects Sant Rajinder Singh's deep wisdom and realizations emerging from divine love and inner fulfillment."

– Deepak Chopra

"A powerful, deep, clearly written book about practical spirituality that helps us let go of the self-made blocks that interfere with the awareness that we are one with God and each other, that there is no separation, and that our soul is present and fully alive forever."

– Gerald G. Jampolsky, M.D., Author of *Love Is Letting Go of Fear*

"Firmly rooted in traditional wisdom, the author faces contemporary questions and challenges squarely and in a non-sectarian way...to bring the seed of peace within us to fruition in daily life and the world we live in."

– Brother David-Steindl Rast

SPARK OF
THE DIVINE

RAJINDER SINGH

RADIANCE PUBLISHERS

Radiance Publishers
1042 Maple Ave.
Lisle, IL 60532
Email: sales@radiancepublishers.com

Publishing History
This edition first published by Radiance Publishers 2011

Second printing: 2011

3   5   7   9   11   13   15   14   12   10   8   6   4   2

© Copyright 2011 Radiance Publishers
Naperville, Illinois, U.S.A.

Library of Congress Control Number: 2011932781

ISBN-13: 978-0-918224-70-5

Printed in Canada by Kromar Press

OTHER BOOKS BY SANT RAJINDER SINGH

Inner and Outer Peace through Meditation

Empowering Your Soul through Meditation

Spiritual Pearls for Enlightened Living

Silken Thread of the Divine

Spiritual Thirst

Echoes of the Divine

Education for a Peaceful World

Visions of Spiritual Unity and Peace

Ecology of the Soul and Positive Mysticism

Vision of the New Millennium

In Hindi:

Spirituality in Modern Times

True Happiness

Self Realization

Search for Peace within the Soul

Salvation through Naam

Spiritual Treasures

Experience of the Soul

Spiritual Talks

ACKNOWLEDGEMENTS

I would like to express my thanks to my revered spiritual Masters, Sant Kirpal Singh Ji Maharaj (1894-1974) and Sant Darshan Singh Ji Maharaj (1921-1989), for their divine grace in illuming the world by awakening seekers to the inner light and sound.

I would like to acknowledge with appreciation my dear wife, Rita Ji, for her love and companionship. I am grateful for the invaluable support and encouragement she has provided over the years and for her dedication and selfless service in the divine work of the Masters.

I would also like to thank Jay and Ricki Linksman for their assistance in the publication of this work.

I offer my eternal gratitude to God, from whom all blessings flow.

DEDICATION

Dedicated to Sant Kirpal Singh Ji Maharaj and Sant Darshan Singh Ji Maharaj who ignited the spark of the Divine in people all over the world so they could experience its loving, blissful luminosity.

TABLE OF CONTENTS

PART I

IGNITING THE FLAME

PART II

MAINTAINING THE FLAME

PART III

THE ETERNAL FLAME

INTRODUCTION

Hidden within each of us is a spark of the Divine. We search for it in the far reaches of the most distant quasars and within the smallest quarks of the atom. Yet, its mysteries lay waiting to be uncovered within us.

This book, *Spark of the Divine*, describes the journey taken to experience the Divine. It is not a gift reserved for the few; it is available to everyone. We have to look within to bask in the eternal sunshine. Through meditation, we can see and hear the light and sound current within. Absorption in this current leads us to experience spiritual realms of consciousness. The meditation technique can be practiced by people of all faiths, countries, and cultures. It does not require any difficult postures or poses. We sit comfortably in the silence of our soul and look within to bask in the wonders of the luminous vistas within. Like a ray of light leads back to the sun, the inner journey leads us to the Source of the current of light and sound, the abode of the Divine. Through meditation, we can merge in that Source and experience infinite consciousness, eternal peace, and never-ending happiness.

This book provides an easy blueprint to spiritual awakening that we can take. Just as we light a fire to warm us without, we need to ignite the spiritual fire within. Once that spark is lit, we need to tend it to keep it glowing. As it illumines us within, we shine forth our eternal light with a luminosity that radiates to all we meet until the entire world is flooded with the light of the Divine and is bathed in eternal love, peace, and bliss.

— Rajinder Singh
August 2011

PART oNE

WITHIN EACH OF US IS a spark of the Divine. Breathtaking regions of beauty, unimaginable vistas of sights and sounds, infinite wisdom, and all-embracing love invite us within. The Light of the Divine glows continually.

Scientists spend billions of dollars looking for our origin

through telescopes scanning the cosmos, or splitting atoms in particle accelerators to find the God-particle. Others seek the Divine through outer practices in all the world's religions. Yet, for most people, the Divine remains a mystery.

In this connection, there is a story of an ancient people who lived before the advent of fire. The only light they knew was the light of the sun in the day, the flickering stars and the ever-changing shape of the moon at night, and the flashes of lightning that frightened and awed them. When night came, their activities ceased. Animals posed a threat in the dark hours. Life was hard.

They had a legend that in the ancient past a great being harnessed the power of the sun. People told stories of this super being to their children, but no one in their lifetimes had ever seen the mysterious flame he had captured.

People would talk about how wonderful life would be if someone could find this flame that would illumine their lives. Yet, they believed that their chances of finding the flame were so remote that they often scoffed at anyone who claimed they could find it. The ruler had offered a valuable reward to anyone who could find this seemingly mythical flame.

One day, a man in that village was bemoaning how poor he was. He had tried eking out a living, but he could not earn enough for himself and his family to make ends meet. He could barely scrape together enough for food and clothing, let alone for the trinkets that wealthier people in his village had.

The man heard the news that the ruler was offering a reward to the one who could find the mysterious flame that could change their people's lives.

He told his family and friends, "I have tried everything to make a good living to support my family. I am going to search for the flame." They thought he was crazy, as no one had ever seen it, and it was considered only a legend.

"Find a more realistic way to make money," his friend told him. "You are going on a wild goose chase if you think you are going to find the flame."

One night, the man had a dream in which a being told him to go into the next kingdom where he would find the flame. The man decided to listen to his dream and undertook the journey to the neighboring kingdom. He had not traveled there before and was unfamiliar with its laws. A guard found him wandering about and brought him to the local prison.

The guard inquired, "What are you doing wandering around day and night?"

The man explained, "I am in search of the legendary flame. I had a dream and I was told I would find it here."

The guard exclaimed, "You are a fool. I have had many dreams about finding the flame. They are only dreams. I ignore them all as they are useless. Once I had a dream that told me to go to a poor, broken-down house in a neighboring village. The house was near a small mountain that had a cave. At the cave's opening was a large rock with a drawing of two sticks. I was told in the dream that I would find the flame there, but I never went there because dreams are not real."

As the guard talked about his dream, the farmer had a shock. The house being described by the guard sounded exactly like his own.

The guard told him, "Go back to your village. You will not find the flame here or anywhere else. It is only a myth."

As the man traveled back to his village, he was overjoyed at the possibility that the flame he was seeking might just be in the mountain cave behind his home.

The man reached home and went to the cave described by the guard. He saw the rock that he had seen there his entire life. He also saw the drawing on the rock of the two sticks. He had always thought the drawing had been scratched there by some children playing years ago, and he had never even wondered if it meant anything.

No one had ever before ventured into the cave, as people feared wild animals might be lurking there. However, enthused by the chance of finding the flame, the man cast all his fears to the wind, and ventured into the cave's opening.

Near the entrance to the cave, in the view of some rays of daylight that streamed in, the man saw some sticks of wood in a heap. Under this heap of wood, he saw some blackened pieces of rock. Suddenly, something caught his eye. It was a small speck of orange that seemed to glow under the rocks. He gently moved the rocks aside, and to his amazement, he saw something he had never seen before in his life. It was a glowing ember of light beneath the black rocks. The sight took him by such surprise that it took his breath away. He then let out a gasp, exclaiming, "Oh, my goodness, this is it!" To better see the light under the ash, he blew on the ember, and suddenly the small spark ignited into a flame. He had travelled far in search of this flame, yet the whole time it was right behind his home.

The man not only had found the flame to claim the ruler's reward and bring wealth to his own family; he had also found the fire that would transform life as his people knew it and illumine the entire world. People would now have fire to brighten their nights, protect them from animals, cook their food, melt iron to form into tools, and make their lives easier. This hidden flame had always been there, but the man had not known where to look.

In the same way, we too have a hidden flame within us that can transform our lives. There is a flame that can empower us with wisdom, eternal happiness, all-embracing love, freedom from fear, and immortality. This flame illumines our heart and mind with answers to questions that have mystified humankind for ages, such as: Why are we here? From where did we come? Where do we go when we die? Like scientists, we search for the answers in the starry skies and in the depths of an atom. We search for the answers in places of worship, in our scriptures, and at places of pilgrimage. Yet we need not search outside to find this wisdom; the flame lies within each of us.

When we uncover that glowing ember, we gaze into the wonders of the Divine and experience beauty, infinite love, unending joy, and unspeakable ecstasy.

This book is a guide to discovering the spark of the Divine within us. In it, we will explore how the spark can be ignited into a fire to transform our lives, how it can be sustained, and how it can be fanned until it glows with infinite brilliance. Just as fire transformed the world, lighting the eternal spark of the Divine within us transforms each of our lives.

PERSONAL REFLECTION

Reflect on your life and on moments when you wondered about the Divine. How would your life be transformed if you could find the eternal flame within you?

2

REALMS OF BEAUTY AND BLISS

Throughout history, the North Star has guided the footsteps of the wayward traveler. So too does the spark of the Divine lead us to self-knowledge and God-realization.

The journey begins by looking inside to find that guiding light of the Divine spark within us. The practice that leads us to that spark is meditation on the inner light and sound.

People of all ages, religions, faiths, and cultures can practice meditation on the inner light and sound. Its simple technique awakens us to the glorious realms of beauty and bliss beyond this physical realm.

Enlightened beings, whether saints, mystics, spiritual Masters, or religious founders, experienced this inner journey and taught their disciples how to travel there as well. For ages, this method was passed on orally from Master to disciple. Masters of the past had a relatively small number of students who learned this technique compared to those in the modern age in which the spiritual floodgates have opened. In the past century alone millions of people have been taught this method to travel to the beyond. In fact, through the wonders of information technology, people wanting to learn this technique are finding out about it through books, radio, television, the Internet, and digital devices of all kinds. It is open to all who seek to undertake this journey.

To travel through the outer cosmos, one boards a spaceship. The fiery combustion of the engines produces lift-off to propel the spacecraft beyond the pull of gravity and into the silent wonders of outer space. To travel into the spiritual realms within, the spark of the Divine is ignited to propel our soul on the inner journey.

A spiritual Master ignites that spark at the time of initiation. Instead of gazing through a spaceship's porthole to see the outer stars and celestial bodies, a spiritual Master teaches a meditation that opens for us an inner porthole. With our spark ignited, our soul begins its wondrous journey to the Divine.

The porthole for our inner journey is situated at a point between and behind the two eyebrows. It is known in various languages as the seat of the soul, single eye, third eye, divya chakshu, tenth door, ajna chakra, or Mount of Transfiguration.

INNER JOURNEY TO
REALMS OF BEAUTY AND BLISS

As we gaze within, we may see a spark of light, flashes of light, pinpoints of light, circles of light, or lights of any color. We may see inner sky, stars, a moon, or a sun within.

As we gaze into what we see within, ultimately we are met by the spiritual Master who has initiated us, who serves as our inner guide through the higher spiritual realms. We may think our earth is large and the solar system still larger. We may think of the entire universe with its solar systems and galaxies as incomprehensibly vast. Yet, this physical realm is small compared to the immensity of the spiritual realms beyond. To think of traveling there alone is daunting; a spiritual guide serves to ensure that we do not get lost in the limitless realms beyond but that we reach our final destination—the Divine who created all these realms.

The journey is filled with wonder, love, bliss, and joy. Our physical eyes may delight in seeing outer beauty, but when we see with our inner eye, it is more than looking at wondrous sights; it is an experience in which we are permeated with the love and bliss emanating from the lights and the celestial music we see and hear within.

To get a small inkling of what the inner journey is like, think about what it feels like to be in love. We may see our beloved with our physical eyes, but we also experience love permeating through us. Similarly, while traversing the inner realms it is more than just a visual experience of seeing sights or an auditory experience of hearing sounds; it is an experience in which we are embraced with a love that wraps our soul in ecstasy.

INTERMEDIARY REGION BETWEEN THE PHYSICAL REALM AND ASTRAL REALM

With the spiritual Master as our guide, we traverse an intermediary region that lies between the physical and astral regions. We soar quickly through this intermediary region with the help of the Master. Those who have had near-death experiences have accessed this intermediary region. When they describe the region of light to which they go when their physical body undergoes clinical death due to an accident or trauma, they are talking about the intermediary region above the physical realm and below the astral realm.

The near-death experience opens up only the borders of the realms beyond, but it has been instrumental in providing overwhelming evidence that there is a beyond. If only one or two people had reported near-death experiences, one might chalk the reports up to a flight of the imagination, but when doctors and medical researchers worldwide have documented case after case, with similar features, it gives pause to reflect on its veracity. In fact, the last Gallup poll on near-death experiences said that around thirteen million people had reported having a near-death experience. Their accounts shared similar features. In fact, people who had never heard of such an experience before they underwent it reported similar characteristics of their journey as the others.

The near-death experience gained publicity in the 1970s with published accounts of people who were declared clinically dead due to an accident or trauma. Yet when revived, they returned to their body and had the same message to report—there is life after this life.

Although numerous books on NDEs have been published since the 1970s, people have been experiencing this phenomenon throughout history. Typical NDEs involve people who, after undergoing clinical death due to an accident or trauma, found themselves hovering above their body, seeing and hearing everything going on in the room. They observed the medical practitioners working on their body. Some of the patients passed through walls and could see and hear relatives talking in the waiting room or even in distant cities. When the patients later were brought back to life and discussed these experiences, the relatives confirmed what the patients saw and heard while lying clinically dead on the operating table.

Next, the people having the NDEs felt themselves rushing through a dark tunnel and emerging into a world of light. The light they encountered was brighter than any light in this physical world, but was not scorching.

Some of them met a being of light who filled them with a love so fulfilling it was unlike any they had experienced on earth. The being embraced them with unconditional love. Many reported how the being of light helped them through a life review in which the memories of all their past thoughts, words, and deeds came back to them. Those who experienced this said it was like watching a three-dimensional movie in which they were simultaneously the main character as well as the observer of their life. They could experience the effect they had had on other people throughout their lives. If they had caused someone pain, they experienced the pain of others. If they had brought joy to someone, they relived that as well. Thus, they became aware of the feelings of others during their life review. The people who underwent this review came to the realization that of all the achievements one could make in this world, love was the most important contribution they could make to help others.

After the life review, they were told they had to return to their physical body to complete the rest of their life. Although the bliss and love they experienced was so wondrous that they did not want to return, they were told they had to go back to Earth. When they returned, they were transformed. They realized the importance of being loving and giving, and they began to change their ways. They learned that our lives are measured not by how much money we make, the extent of our name and fame, the possessions we amass, or our intelligence and skills, but by the love, service, sacrifice, and goodness we do. What is valued in the beyond is how much we love others. When those having NDEs returned to life, they realized that the secret to making the world a better place was through love.

A significant feature of these accounts of NDE's is that they confirm what mystics, saints, founders of the different religions, and spiritual Masters have been saying through the ages when they have described mystic lands beyond. Unfortunately, mechanistic science had dashed the faith of millions of people in the modern age, causing them to doubt the teachings of their own religions. If the experiences described in the scriptures could not be duplicated in a laboratory setting and measured by instrumentation, they were debunked. Thus, many people lost belief in the afterlife, in heaven, in the soul, and even in God. These near-death experiences, reported by those who have been tested to be rational and normal people and who are often professionals in many fields, including medicine, psychiatry, education, and the sciences, have helped to reestablish belief in mystic lands beyond.

Since each of us will ultimately journey to these mystic lands after death and will reside there for a much longer time than we would have spent in our temporary residency on earth, it may behoove us to look into what awaits us. The fear that grips us when we think of our own mortality or that of our loved ones can be calmed when we glimpse during our lifetime what awaits us after this life ends.

Accounts of near-death experiences confirm what teachers of Sant Mat through the centuries have taught and continue to teach. We are soul, drops of the Creator. In the divine plan, numerous regions were created and souls were sent to inhabit these worlds. Souls have been sent out by the Divine and ultimately will return to the Divine.

If those who had a near-death experience describe such tremendous joy and peace that they did not want to return to this physical world, but returned as it was not yet their time to physically die, one can imagine how great was the love and bliss. Their near-death experience of the loving light and peace at the end of the tunnel where they emerged into a world of light is the threshold of still higher realms.

One does not need to undergo a physical trauma or near-death experience to reach the higher realms. In meditation, the spiritual guide takes us higher and still higher without us having the ordeal of a physical accident that those who had NDEs experienced. Meditation is a blissful process from which we return to our awareness of the body whenever we want.

VISIT TO THE ASTRAL REALM

Passing beyond the intermediary region, we enter the astral realm. We are greeted by a myriad of brilliant lights of colors not even known to us in the physical realm. They sparkle with a light more dazzling than diamonds, rubies, or emeralds of this world. The music resounding in this realm is indescribable. The intensity of the sound that fills our soul with uplifting bliss is beyond any sounds we know in the physical realm. One can think about the difference between high-definition digital surround-sound and the flat monaural records people played on record players of the past. This difference helps us imagine how if we took the best recording of the music of this physical world and stepped it up to a higher level of vibration, it would just give an inkling of how much more ethereal and indescribable is the inner sound in the realms beyond.

The astral realm is only the beginning of the inner journey. Inhabitants of this realm exist in an astral body, an ethereal form that radiates light. Without a physical body, we can travel through the astral realm by desires and wishes. We are not constrained by having to drag a body around, so we can travel at the speed of our desires to wherever we wish. We may think the astral realm is amazing, but it is still limited compared to the higher realms. The astral realm is made of matter with more consciousness than the physical realm, but there are still more ethereal regions awaiting us.

With all its lands and continents, the astral realm is still subject to our mind. It is a realm in which we can materialize any of our thoughts and desires. Thus, just as the physical realm binds us by our worldly attachments and keeps us from knowing the Divine, we can become waylaid and distracted by the astral realm. Like a child in a toyshop, we may enjoy materializing whatever we want and become absorbed in these manifestations, but we miss the point of our inner journey: reaching the highest realm of eternal love and bliss, the Divine Creator.

A spiritual Master as our inner guide keeps us focused on our journey so we are not distracted by sightseeing in this realm. The Master wants us to pass through this realm quickly so we can enjoy still higher realms of joy and ecstasy. As delightful as the astral realm is, sightseeing there is as fruitless as it is in this physical world. It excites our curiosity and amazes our astral mind, but it does not provide us with lasting happiness and divine love. There are much higher delights waiting in the regions beyond the astral.

NEXT STOP: THE CAUSAL REALM

Our next stop on the journey to the Divine is the causal realm. If we thought the astral realm was incredibly beautiful, the astral region pales in comparison to the causal realm. This realm is made of equal parts matter and consciousness. This makes it even more ethereal than the astral realm. The lights of the causal realm are far brighter and more luminous. The music is more enchanting. The causal realm is vaster than the astral realm. It has incredible continents with unimaginably high mountains, cascading rivers and an ocean of light, sights, and sounds inconceivable to our physical mind.

In each realm there are throngs of souls engaged in all sorts of pursuits. In the causal realm, we can move without our physical and astral bodies and journey at the speed of thought. Whatever we think can manifest. We can travel anywhere in this realm instantly. It is also a realm in which we can see our past lives, a realm in which all the records of all our past lives are stored. Thus, we can trace back the history of our karma and see how it influenced all our lives.

The Master, though, does not want us distracted from our inner journey to the Divine by having us delve into our past lives. Think of this distraction as trying to make it to the airport for our flight to take a journey, but before we leave the house, we find a photo album of our life. It contains our baby pictures through our toddler years, teen years, young adult years, and recent times, along with a written description of every day of our lives. Then imagine there were albums of photos with biographies for all our past lives. If we started going through them all, we would miss our flight. It could take us years and decades to go through all our past stories of previous lives. The Master does not let us linger here on the causal region as there are still more realms to visit with even more love and bliss.

BATHE IN THE CLEANSING LAKE OF THE MANSAROVAR IN THE SUPRACAUSAL REALM

The Master next takes us to the supracausal realm. This is a grand leap for we leave behind the realms controlled by the mind. The physical, astral, and causal realms are under the control of the universal mind. The mind is what keeps us distracted in the lower realms, whether physical, astral, or causal. It prevents us from knowing ourselves in our true state as the soul and from knowing the Divine Creator, God.

Because the pull of the mind is so great, we need a spiritual Master to help us transcend the three lower realms of the mind. As a spaceship needs tremendous force to escape the gravitational pull of the earth to reach outer space, our soul needs the spiritual radiation of a Master to help us rise out of the realms controlled by the pull of the mind.

Here we find a pool of nectar, called the Mansarovar, in which the soul bathes and sheds its causal body. The soul is now covered only with a thin veil. This region is beyond the mind and senses. There is absolutely no physical language that can even give us an inkling of what the supracausal realm is like. We have only pale analogies. Since the physical, astral, and causal minds have been left behind in the lower worlds, mind is of no use to us here. This realm is directly experienced by the soul with only a thin covering. The supracausal realm also has its own distinguishing light and sound that helps the soul recognize where it is. It is in this realm that the soul, losing the forgetfulness that limited it in the lower realms, cries out "Sohang," or "I am That." It realizes, "I am the same essence as God."

The supracausal is a realm of mostly consciousness with only a thin layer of illusion. The Mansarovar lake is filled with *hansas*, meaning purified souls, delighting in the joy of realizing their true nature. The soul, stripped of its covering of the mind, realizes that its true essence is the same as God. We experience that as soul we shine with a brilliant light. We realize that the suns and stars of the physical worlds are but pale reflections of the inner lights of the higher realms and of our own soul.

The supracausal realm is beyond description. Everything we know in our physical, astral, and causal realms is a manifestation of the mind. In realms beyond the mind, there is no frame of reference or words to convey what it is like. It is like trying to describe colors to a person who cannot see or music to a person who cannot hear. It is experienced as transcendent love, blissful beyond comprehension. Everything is experienced by the soul without the handicap of the mind's constraints.

Even in the physical realm, words cannot capture certain experiences. For example, language cannot convey the enjoyment, flavor, and sweetness of ice cream to one who has never tasted it. If we only read about what it is like we miss savoring the flavor for ourselves. We can also compare the experience of feeling love for someone to only reading about love. In the same way, the soul can experience bliss, love, and beauty of the higher realms without the involvement of the mind and the limitations of language.

The supracausal is not, however, a realm of feelings. Rather, it is a realm of bliss experienced by our soul beyond emotions and feelings. Feelings are limited as they are only experienced at the level of our mind. We can feel happiness, or its opposite, unhappiness. However, bliss has no opposite. Bliss is an eternal state of God and the soul. It resides at our true core. It does not change, but is an ever-present state we experience when we realize ourselves as soul. Feelings come and go as do waves in the ocean, catapulting us from highs to lows. If we get what we want we are happy; if we do not get what we want we are sad. Bliss is not dependent on the outer circumstances of life. When we strip our soul of the covering of the mind and enter the supracasaul realm, we experience true bliss.

THE FINAL DESTINATION: THE UNENDING LOVE OF THE PURELY SPIRITUAL REALM OF THE DIVINE

The supracausal realm is not the end of the journey. The Master does not want us to linger here because the next phase of the journey is our ultimate destination—the purely spiritual realm known as Sach Khand or Sat Lok (True Home or True Realm). This region, beyond the mind and intellect, is where the soul experiences its true nature and returns to its Source, God. Here, bliss and love surpass those experienced in all the realms below it. Sach Khand is the realm of all spirit with no matter or illusion. This is the luminous and infinite realm of the Divine. In Sach Khand, its true Home, the soul fully merges into the Divine.

The light of Sach Khand is beyond those of all the other realms. Millions of outer suns of this physical realm would not equal even one small portion of the Divine in Sach Khand. How intensely bright is that? Think of the difference between the light of a candle and the light of the sun. Scientists speak of the light of the sun as being dim compared to the light of distant quasars. Similarly, the lights of this physical realm are but dark and dim compared to the light of God radiating without any covering in the realm of Sach Khand.

With all the intensity with which a worldly lover rushes into the arms of its beloved and consummates their love, so does the soul rush into the arms of the Divine in Sach Khand. Like a magnet, the soul is pulled to reunite with God. The joys of the supracausal realm reach an even greater intensity beyond any human description when we enter Sach Khand. Pure light and sound bathe us and the soul shines with the brilliance of sixteen outer suns. Our soul fully and completely merges in God. We experience the exhilaration and joyousness of our own true state. There is no pain, no sorrow, and no death. All is peace and perpetual happiness. Overwhelming love and unending bliss is ours when we merge back in God. God is love. In Sach Khand, we become one with the ocean of love. As God is consciousness, when we merge in God we become all conscious. It is an enrapturing ecstasy beyond comprehension. The spark of light merges with the light and becomes the light. We are finally fulfilled.

TECHNIQUE OF MEDITATION ON
THE INNER LIGHT AND SOUND

Saints do not want us only to read about these descriptions in a book; they want us to experience all of these higher realms for ourselves. It is only by experiencing them that we prove to ourselves their existence. One reason why the saints do not dwell on describing these realms is that they want us to see them ourselves. They say, "Seeing is above all." The goal of the saints is to show us how to reach these realms. They want us to enter through the inner porthole so we can know for certain what lies beyond.

FINDING THIS PORTHOLE TO BEGIN
OUR INNER VOYAGE

Meditation on the inner light and sound helps us find this doorway. To meditate, we sit in a comfortable pose, most convenient to us, in which we can sit still for the longest possible time. We take our attention from the body, where we are aware of our feet, legs, hands, torso, etc., and raise it to the seat of the soul between and behind the two eyebrows. Movement brings our attention back down into our body, distracting us from concentration on the seat of the soul. We need to sit comfortably to give our attention the time needed to rise to the seat of the soul.

We close our eyes gently as we do when we go to sleep, but we remain wide awake. This keeps us from being distracted by the outer sights of the physical world. We do not put pressure on our eyes. We also do not raise our eyes upwards towards the direction of the eyebrows as that tension can result in a headache. Rather, we keep our gaze focused gently in front of us and look into the middle of what appears within. We keep gazing horizontally, focusing about eight to ten inches in front of us with closed eyes.

We look lovingly into the middle of what appears in front of us. We may at first see either a field of darkness or a field of light, sparks of light, pinpoints of light, flashes of light, circles of light, or light of any color, such as golden, white, yellow, orange, red, purple, violet, blue, or green. No matter what we see, we continue to gaze into the middle of what appears.

We may see inner vistas such as inner sky, clouds, stars, a moon, or a sun. These may lead to the inner radiant form of our spiritual Master, who serves as our guide to take us on an incredible inner journey beyond this physical realm.

While gazing into the middle of what appears, we may notice that our mind distracts us with thoughts. We may find that the thoughts distract us from gazing within. We may find that we cannot silence our mind to continue meditating. The Masters provide a remedy for us. At the time of initiation, the spiritual Master gives us five charged Words to repeat mentally to keep our attention focused on gazing.

These Words go on mentally, as we continue to gaze. Concentrating at the third eye causes the sensory currents to withdraw. These sensory currents are usually spread out in the body and make us aware of our bodily sensation. As the sensory currents withdraw, we are no longer distracted by the feelings in our feet, legs, arms, hands, or torso. As our attention converges at the third eye, we then see the inner light. By gazing deeper into the middle of that light, the soul rises into the spiritual realms. The Master then takes us on the journey within.

JOURNEY OF MEDITATION: AN INSTANT VACATION FROM STRESS AND PROBLEMS

This journey is like having an instant vacation from the tensions and strains of life. A vacation offers a chance to take a break from the stresses of daily living. We usually seek places that are relaxing, enjoyable, and beautiful. Yet, going on an outer vacation is often stressful. We have to earn money for the trip; book tickets; undergo the rigors of travel, whether by road, train, bus, or air; find the right accommodations and food service; and face unexpected inclement weather. Often, we return from a vacation more exhausted than when we left.

What if we could experience a vacation that did not cost anything and in which we could instantly travel to and experience unimaginable vistas more beautiful than anything ever seen in this world? What if that vacation filled us with relaxation of our body, mind, and spirit, and had the added benefit of putting us into states of tremendous love, joy, and bliss? What if we could tap into a restful peace that washed away our troubles and stayed with us even when we returned from the journey? What if we could take this trip anytime we wanted, as many times as we wished, by just closing our eyes? This is not science fiction, as shown on the "Star Trek" television program, where the space crew could travel instantly by saying, "Beam me up, Scottie," and their bodies would disappear in one place and reappear in another. This journey is not imaginary. Many enlightened beings, saints, mystics, religious founders, and spiritual Masters and their disciples have taken this inner voyage. Through the ages, the spiritual journey was largely a mystery to the masses, but was known to disciples through an oral tradition whereby Masters passed on the travel directions for this journey. This experience is still available today to all who want to undertake this incredible voyage. It is a journey that begins with finding the spark within and following its rays to the Divine.

Sightseeing in this physical world may attract our senses with interesting and beautiful sights, sounds, smells, tastes, and feelings. Yet, inner sightseeing dazzles us with lights more luminous than even the brightest stars and suns in the physical universe. We witness colors unknown to our physical eyes. The inner music makes the most beautiful orchestral performances of this world sound flat and dull. The inner voyage thrills our soul with bliss, love, and joy that far surpass any sensory delights experienced in this physical world. The culmination of the spiritual journey is the ecstasy of union as the spark merges back into the eternal flame of the Divine.

PERSONAL REFLECTION

Think about what it would mean for your life if you were to undertake the inner journey and experience the bliss and love of the Divine awaiting within.

3

SPARK OF THE DIVINE

The latent spark of the Divine is within each human being. It awaits a catalyst to ignite it so its brilliant flame can be actualized.

The principles of spirituality work like the scientific laws that govern our planet. The same laws that work in our universe are reflections of those that govern the higher realms of creation. The principles at work both in the physical and spiritual realms can help us understand how a spiritual Master serves as a catalyst to ignite our spark within. Once that spark is lit, its radiant light becomes visible when we invert our attention during meditation. We receive a firsthand experience of what lies beyond and attain knowledge of our true selves and realize God.

THE CATALYST

How does a spiritual Master light the spark in us? To understand this process, think of how scientists and engineers in this physical realm connect sources of power and energy to people's homes. Engineers devise systems in which electrical energy from a power plant is channeled to a home for many purposes, such as heating, cooling, lighting, and running appliances and technological gadgets. An engineer or scientist knows how to hook up the end users to the source of energy. They make new connections and fix broken ones.

Specialists connect radios to radio waves, televisions to broadcast signals, and computers to networks to help us communicate through email and the Internet.

Making connections to receive electronic or digital signals in this physical realm is analogous to making connections between the soul and God. For both, we need a sender and a receiver. The divine sender is the Lord. The receiver of God's broadcast is our soul. The Master is a specialist who makes the connection so our soul can be receptive to messages from God.

We need such a specialist because God's messages come through only as spirit and do not involve any matter. Since the receiver in the physical body is the brain and senses made of matter, it is limited to only receiving communications from the material world. Our eyes can only pick up light of certain wavelengths: red, orange, yellow, green, blue, and violet. Some instrumentation can pick up wavelengths of higher and lower frequencies such as ultraviolet and infrared waves. Beyond those wavelengths, our eyes and scientific instrumentation are unequipped for reception. Although higher spiritual frequencies are always being transmitted, we are unable to receive them through our physical senses.

Similarly, the human ear can only hear certain sound frequencies. Some animals, such as the dog or whale, can respond to a wider range of frequencies in this world. Our physical ears, though, are ill equipped to pick up spiritual frequencies of higher sounds emanating from God.

We also respond to certain smells, tastes, and physical sensations through our senses. That is the extent of our ability to receive communication at the physical level.

SPIRITUAL RECEIVER

God is spirit. Unfortunately, the physical instruments of the body cannot pick up God's spiritual messages. To receive spiritual communication from the Divine, we need to be in tune with another system of reception, known as the soul. The soul, made of spirit, is attuned to spiritual vibrations and can receive communication from God.

The soul can receive communication from regions beyond the physical realm. Meditation opens us up to the higher vibrations from these realms. Our soul is really not traveling in physical space during meditation. We talk about "higher" realms, but they do not exist in a vertical progression through space as we know it on earth. Rather, all the regions exist concurrently and only differ in their level of vibration. Each region, whether physical, astral, causal, supracausal, or the spiritual realm of Sach Khand, has a different vibratory rate. In meditation, we attune to the higher vibrations to experience each realm. The Master is the catalyst that tunes our attention to these higher vibrations.

The physical realm is made predominantly of matter with a small amount of consciousness, which is the soul within each of us. The astral realm is made of matter but with more consciousness or spirit than that which exists in the physical realm. When our soul transcends physical consciousness to the astral realm, we experience that realm through awareness of our astral body and astral mind. The astral body and mind can perceive and interact with the astral realm.

Similarly, we experience the causal realm, which contains equal parts of consciousness and matter, through our causal body and causal mind. When our soul rises to the causal realm, it functions in the causal body and causal mind so it can receive communication from the causal realm.

Beyond these three lower realms of matter are the spiritual realms. The supracausal realm is mostly spirit with only a veil of illusion. We experience the supracausal realm with our soul, covered by a thin veil. The higher vibratory rate of the soul with this veil helps us perceive and interact with the supracausal realm.

We experience the realm of Sach Khand, which is all spirit with no matter, through the soul with all coverings removed. In this realm, the soul recognizes its true nature as spirit as a part of God. Here, the soul's vibratory rate is the same as God's, and it achieves oneness with God. The soul communicates directly with God. In this state, we attain God-consciousness.

The system is scientific and works perfectly. If we can identify with our soul we can be attuned to communication with God. The question is, "What is the catalyst that can reunite the spark with the Divine from which it emanated?"

A CATALYST IGNITES OUR SPARK

The catalyst that ignites our spark to connect with the Divine is a divine Engineer. Right now there is static interfering with the connection between the soul and God. We cannot communicate with God because on our own we do not know how to eliminate the interference to open the lines of communication. Just as we are untrained to connect a radio station with a radio or a computer with the Internet, similarly, we are untrained to connect our spark to the Divine. To make the connection between our soul and God, we need training. We need to call someone who is computer literate to hook us up to the Internet. We need to call a cable technician to hook our television to cable TV. In the field of spirituality, if we were able to connect our soul to God ourselves, each would have done so by now. Yet, few people know how to do it. To connect with God, we need an expert. That person who can make that connection for us is a spiritual Master.

A spiritual Master teaches a form of meditation that does more than help us feel peaceful and calm; he connects our soul with God. The meditation connects us to a current of light and sound emanating from God that is already re-verberating within us. We just need to learn how to tap into it to see and hear it. A Master is a catalyst who makes that internal connection for us. He teaches us how to meditate to stay in tune with the light and sound current, which takes us through the astral, causal, and supracausal regions until the soul merges back with God in Sach Khand.

The divine Engineer attunes our instrument—the soul—to receive the spiritual communication from God. As in science, the process must be done correctly to work. Even in the worldly sphere, when we go to a teacher, there is an understanding that the teacher has something to offer the student. It may be intellectual knowledge or career training. It could be techniques of playing a sport or skills in the performing arts. Any student who goes to an instructor and is eager and ready to learn will gain something. However, if a student is egotistical and thinks he or she knows more than the teacher, little will be gained. When we have the attitude that we have nothing to learn, we close ourselves off from receiving what the teacher has to give. We then remain at a standstill as far as our own development is concerned.

The great scientist Isaac Newton once spoke of the vastness of knowledge. He remarked that he was just picking up pebbles from the seashore of time. If such an intellectual giant as Newton felt as if he were still a student with much more to learn, then how can anyone of lesser stature feel so proud of his or her learning?

There is an anecdote about former United States President Teddy Roosevelt. He was a great nature lover. In the evenings, he would spend time talking with a friend, and afterwards they would take a walk together. One night, as they went for a walk, they looked up at the starry night sky. They noticed how vast space was and how many stars there were. They looked with wonder at the Milky Way, the Big Dipper, the Little Dipper, and the vastness of space, and were in such awe that they walked in silence.

Finally, Teddy Roosevelt spoke what both of them had on their mind, saying, "Well, I think we are small enough now. Let's call it a night."

Most people act and feel as if the whole universe circles around them. In reality, we are a small part of the whole. When our heads become swollen, thinking we are better than everyone else including God, we can no longer be open to learning and receiving. We become small and congealed and do not learn and grow.

To increase knowledge, sharpen our skills, and improve our techniques in any worldly field, we need to be open to receive what the instructor has to give. This principle is equally valid when we look at the spiritual sciences. When we go to a spiritual Adept to learn how to realize ourselves and realize God, we need to approach him with a willingness to learn. What a Master has to give is unique. It is not available from anyone else in this world. From all other instructors we gain exoteric knowledge, which is knowledge of the outer world. From a Master we gain esoteric knowledge, or knowledge of the inner world.

The Master is a catalyst that connects us to the spark of the Divine. When performing certain scientific experiments, we add a catalyst to cause a chemical reaction; similarly, the Master is a catalyst that makes the connection between our soul with God. The process by which he makes that connection to experience the light and sound of God within us is called initiation. At initiation, he opens our inner eye to see the light of God and opens our inner ear to hear the sound of God within. He gives us a spiritual boost so we can withdraw our attention from the body to focus at the single or third eye between and behind the two eyebrows to experience inner light. We become absorbed into the light and witness inner vistas such as flashes of light, pinpoints of light, lights of various colors and the inner sky, stars, a moon, and a sun. That boost then leads us to the radiant or ethereal form of the Master, who serves as our inner Guide. In the presence of the radiant form we travel beyond the physical realm to experience the astral, causal, and supracausal realms, until we merge back in God in the highest spiritual realm of Sach Khand.

Souls experience upliftment to reconnect with God in two ways: through the radiation of a Master that emanates from his physical presence, and through his charged attention sent to us even from around the world. Those who are receptive receive the full dose of divinity whether in his presence of not. The spiritual boost from either his physical presence when in his company or from his charged attention we receive in meditation helps us enjoy inner experiences. The emptier we are of distracting thoughts during our meditation, the greater the benefit we receive from a Master, because we are open to receive the spiritual radiation.

We can receive the spiritual boost from the Master through his eyes. That glance is called the darshan of the Master. It is so powerful it can uplift our soul to the third eye to connect with the light and sound within. The glance of grace gives more bliss than intoxicating drugs and alcohol and has no harmful side effects to our body, mind, society, or relationships. Physical intoxicants may temporarily make us forget our pains, but when these wear off, we need another fix. The spiritual intoxication of a glance of grace uplifts us immediately and takes us to a state of consciousness higher than any we can reach in this world. It takes us to a state of bliss more intense than any in this physical realm.

Through his charged attention, we can receive that glance directly whether in his presence or during meditation even when we are physically ten thousand miles away from him, because that glance is not emanating from the physical form of the Master. The charging is coming from the Divine through the catalyst of the Master. The beauty of this glance is that it stays with us. It is free and available to us anytime we go within during mediation.

The Master is not the physical body, but a catalyst through which the Divine can flow to us. It is always radiating divine love. We can experience that power of divine love when we turn our attention from the world to the channel of God within. The Master is that divine Engineer, who through the glance of grace, helps us switch our channel from the world outside to God within. On our own, we are tuned out. If we are open to receive the spiritual radiation and the glance of grace of the Master, we will become tuned in to the channel of God. Through initiation by a spiritual Master, the spark of the Divine is ignited so that through meditation on the light and sound current we journey through higher spiritual realms until our soul reconnects with God.

PERSONAL REFLECTION

Think of how teachers or coaches have helped you in various fields of life. Reflect on whether you are ready to benefit from having a spiritual Master.

PART
TWO

4

KEEPING
THE FLAME
BURNING BRIGHTLY

ONCE A FIRE IS IGNITED, it needs to be maintained to keep it burning brightly. One needs to tend and protect it to prevent it from going out. Similarly, once our spiritual spark is ignited, it needs to be tended. It requires attention and maintenance, as many forces can pull our focus from keeping the spiritual flame burning. Helping factors to keep the spark glowing so we can successfully reunite our soul with the eternal Flame of the Divine include: ethical living, a vegetarian diet, selfless service, and spiritual upliftment.

When a lit candle is placed in a glass candleholder, if the glass is not kept clean the light cannot shine forth in all its brilliance. When we turn on a lamp, if the dust has not been kept off the bulb the light will appear dim. Similarly, the spark of light within us needs to be kept free from the layers of dust and grime that can cover it.

What sullies the glass? Since the soul began its journey, the dust and grime of our negative thoughts, words, and deeds have accumulated and dimmed its light.

The spiritual path is a process of reuniting our soul with God. Although the soul and God are already knit together, we cannot recognize our union. The situation is like a husband and wife who share the same bed but cannot see each other. Similarly, although the soul and God both reside together within us, our soul cannot see God. Why? Our interior room is cluttered with mess and grime. If we could clean the chamber, we would find that God is already within us. Meditation and ethical living lead to cleaning the chamber of our heart.

KEEPING THE GLASS CLEAN

There are simple steps we can take to keep the covering over our soul clean. A spiritual Master gives the secret for success on the spiritual path. First, we should meditate. Second, an ethical life protects us from accumulating layers of grime that block the brilliant light of our soul. For this, a Master provides us an introspection diary to help us eliminate any blockages so our flame can glow brightly.

Saint Tulsi Sahib of India wrote a beautiful verse describing how to keep our soul clear of grime. This verse, which contains the essence of success on the spiritual path, says:

Cleanse the chamber of your heart
for the Beloved to come;
Remove your attention from others
if you want it on the Beloved.

What is cluttering the chamber of our heart? Several impediments block our vision of God. First, loads of dirt have piled up from ages of accumulated karma. Second, negative thoughts, words, and deeds swirl through our system. Third, our desires keep our attention on worldly attainments rather than on God.

VISION BLOCKED BY PAST KARMAS

The first impediment to keeping our vision clear is our past karma. We have to wind up our past karmas for the soul to reunite with God. In each life, we engage in thoughts, words, and deeds for which we are held accountable. Some are good and some are negative. These result in reactions—either a reward for good thoughts, words, and deeds; or an undesirable consequence for bad thoughts, words, and deeds. These karmic debts must be paid. If not paid by the end of our life, leftover karma goes into a storehouse. From that storehouse, called sanchit karma, a portion is taken out as karmas that must be paid in a particular future life. Those earmarked for a particular life are called our fate, destiny karma, or pralabdh karma. These determine the events in that particular life. While paying off past karma, we are also accumulating new karma each day, called kriyaman karma.

These also add up in our karmic account. Thus, our room is filled with sanchit karma; pralabdh karma, which is the portion of our storehouse karma allotted for this life; and our new kriyaman karma. For God to be seen within the chamber of our heart, these karmas must be cleaned up.

VISION BLOCKED BY
THOUGHTS, WORDS, AND DEEDS

The second impediment to keeping our vision clear is that we fill every moment with thoughts, words, and deeds. Whether good or bad, these fully occupy our attention. We can only see God when the glass is cleaned of all thoughts, words, and deeds. Until we eliminate these, we only see layers covering the light. There are so many of these thoughts, it is hard to focus on God. The way to clean the glass covering our soul is by eliminating thoughts, words, and deeds that keep us from seeing God.

Life is difficult. Many situations upset us, and we wonder how we can remain ethical in the face of these daily challenges. We must choose how to deal with these situations. At each moment we are confronted with choices between right and wrong. For example, we are surrounded by people in our home, at work, and in the community. Whenever there are other people involved, there are bound to be situations where others are doing things with which we disagree. Everyone is trying to live out his or her own life, and sometimes there are clashes between what others want and what we want. Some people may be violent, and others may be untruthful. Some people may be greedy and selfish, while others may try to take advantage of us. As we walk down the pathway of life, we encounter all sorts of people. Walking the spiritual path is like walking on a razor's edge because we have to navigate through all these difficult situations and still maintain our spiritual values and principles. There are many pitfalls along the way into which one can fall. Although the spiritual path is straight and narrow, if followed it leads directly to self-knowledge and God-realization.

In this connection, there is a story about a good, compassionate man. He was sitting along a riverbank, when he spotted a scorpion being carried away by the rushing waters.

The man had a good and compassionate heart and thought, "That poor scorpion is struggling in the water. If I don't help him, he will drown." The man dove into the water towards the scorpion and grabbed hold of the creature to save its life.

While the man held the scorpion safely in his hand, the scorpion stung him. The man yelled out, and as a natural reaction pulled his hand back. It opened and the scorpion fell out of his hand back into the rushing river. As the scorpion was again being swept away, the man forgot his own pain and thought of how the poor scorpion would drown. The man again swam down the river toward the scorpion to save him from drowning. The man reached the scorpion, took hold of him, and tried to carry him to safety along the riverbank. Again, the scorpion stung his hand. As a reaction, the man yelled and pulled back his hand and the scorpion ended up back in the river.

The man called to it, "I just saved your life from drowning twice. Why do you keep stinging me?"

The scorpion said, "I stung you because that is what scorpions do." The man was in pain and felt bad that he was stung, but still felt sorry for the scorpion's plight and wanted to save him again.

The scorpion called back to the man, "If you know I will keep stinging you, why do you keep trying to save me?"

The man replied to the scorpion, "Because I am a good person who feels compassion for others and have forgiven you, and that is what good people do!"

For those on the spiritual path, this story has a strong message. Some people are still slaves to their passions. They do not try to improve themselves by developing ethical virtues. They may hurt others or be untruthful, egotistical, or selfish. They have not yet realized the value of ethical living and of purifying themselves to take steps back to God. Until they tread the spiritual path they remain unaware of the consequences of leading an unethical life. Every day we encounter such people. Without a reason to change their ways, they keep doing things that are harmful to themselves and to others.

On the other hand, we who are walking on the spiritual path are trying to perfect our ethical way of living. We are trying to be nonviolent, truthful, pure, humble, and selfless. Our challenge is to act virtuously even in the face of people who sting us like scorpions. We need to be like the good man in the story who continued to do good no matter how he was treated. This story is a reminder that no matter how badly other people may act, we can choose to remain good.

It is difficult to remain nonviolent in the face of violence. It is difficult to remain truthful in the face of untruth. It is difficult to remain humble in the face of ego. It is difficult to remain selfless in the face of selfishness. It is difficult to remain pure in the face of impurity. Each day we are faced with challenges. We want to be vegetarian and avoid drugs and alcohol, but nonvegetarian food, drugs, and alcohol saturate modern society. We want to meditate, but there are numerous interruptions and distractions to keep us from meditating. The challenge on the spiritual path is to choose what is good in the face of choices that are bad for us.

We need to be like a tree that can grow strong in the soil despite the elements around it. When a young tree is planted, a small fence or wooden stakes are planted around it to keep it safe from animals or winds that can knock it down. We need a small fence around ourselves so our budding spiritual growth can flourish. In this way, it will not be knocked down by winds that keep us from our goal. Within that fence, we need to be nourished by the nutrients of meditation and ethical living. We should stay focused on these activities so no outside elements can deter us from growing spiritually. Thus, we can remain safe from falling prey to negative characteristics. If people try to knock us down from being nonviolent, truthful, pure, humble, and selfless, or try to distract us from our meditations, we should remain firm. No matter how many times others sting us, as the scorpion did in the story, we should continue to be the good, compassionate people we are. Just as the man forgave the scorpion and continued to be a good man, we should continue to maintain our ethical values in spite of what happens to us.

God sees everything that we and others do. All is recorded in our karmic accounts. Why should we delay our own progress and add to our own karma through our thoughts, words, and deeds because of what others have done? No matter what happens, we should not give up our goodness.

Failures in each virtue can sully our glass. For example, anger and violence need to be eliminated. Anger is usually toward another person. When angry, we think about that person and what he or she did or said. We review what happened between us. We replay the scenario, as if replaying a movie. We may even invent scenarios of how to get back at that person. We may plan future words or actions about how to seek revenge. How can the divine Beloved make himself known to us when we are filled with thoughts of another person? Before the Beloved can be known to us, we must stop thinking about other people and what they have done to us.

To stop thinking of those who hurt us, we must let go of anger. To clean our house of anger we can ask ourselves, "Do I want to spend my time interacting angrily with the other person through my thoughts, words, and deeds, or would I rather experience my Beloved?" When we gain spiritual wisdom, we decide, "I do not want to waste my time with angry thoughts of others. I want to open myself up for the Beloved to enter the chamber of my heart." By doing this, we are no longer engaged in thoughts of anger, for we are busy thinking of the Beloved God.

Violence includes harming other people or animals. God is within each living creature, whether animal, bird, fish, reptile, or insect. A life of nonviolence means not taking the life of any creature. To practice a nonviolent life, a prerequisite for those seeking initiation into the inner light and sound is to maintain a strict vegetarian diet in which meat, fish, fowl, and eggs are avoided. A vegetarian diet is one in which we live on plants, such as vegetables, fruits, grains, nuts, seeds, beans, and legumes. It can also include milk and dairy products. In ancient India, milking a cow was a natural process that did not harm the cow, so dairy products were permitted by saints for those who wished to be initiated into the spiritual path.

Next, we must eliminate greed. Being greedy means that we want to gain more and more material belongings. It includes possessiveness in which we want to control other people and tell them what to think, say, and do. How can the Beloved enter when we are filled with greed? The Beloved is trying to come into our home, but it is cluttered with belongings. We are either occupied with thoughts of amassing more wealth, luxuries, and possessions; or we are occupied with thinking of ways to make other people give us what we want. Unless we get rid of thoughts of greed, the Beloved has no space to enter us.

We also have to rid ourselves of lust. Lust and love are different. Love is a meeting of two hearts. We exchange love from eyes to eyes, from heart to heart, and from soul to soul. Love is a merging of the inner essence of two souls. Love is when two become one. It is a mutual relationship in which two souls express love, affection, caring, and appreciation for each other. Lust sees others as objects to use for its own benefit. If that is where our attention is, then how can the Beloved, who is spirit, be comfortable within us when our mind is filled with lust for something or someone of this world? Our attention then is not on the Beloved, but on a worldly person. The Masters describe how lust pulls our attention into the world. If we want our attention to move towards God, then we should replace lust with love. The highest love is love for the Divine.

We must also clean our glass of attachment. Any thoughts of attachment to anything or anybody of this world will block out our Beloved. The Beloved wants to be known by us, but how can that happen, when our heart and mind are cluttered with thoughts of and attachment to our possessions or other people? We need to loosen our attachments and clean them out. When we realize that everything to which we are attached is temporary and will one day be taken from us, we will loosen our attachment to them. If we are attached to wealth or belongings, we should realize that we could lose them in a moment's notice due to a catastrophe, either through financial loss or natural disaster. If we are attached to people, we should realize that one day they will leave us or die, or we will die. The relationships of the world are not lasting. If we instead attach ourselves to the Divine, who is eternal, we will be saved from the pain of loss when we lose our worldly attachments. Once we rid ourselves of worldly attachment, the Beloved can be known by us.

The hardest failure to clean out of all the virtues is ego. Ego is so difficult to remove that even yogis meditating in the jungle for years have a hard time letting go of it. When filled with ego, we are filled with thoughts of our own selves. We compare ourselves to others. When we are egotistical, we feel that we are better than everyone else.

Ego is subtle. We may be a victim of pride concerning power, wealth, or knowledge. Pride of power or position means we think we are more powerful than others. This is reflected by our words and actions in which we feel we are the big bosses and others must cater to us. Ego makes us tell everyone what to do.

Pride of wealth means we feel entitled to whatever we want and everyone else must do our bidding. We feel that because we have more money, others should be subservient to us. We feel special because we are affluent.

Pride of knowledge means we feel we are intellectually superior to everyone else. We feel we are smart and everyone else is not as intelligent. We think that our ideas are better than everyone else's. It may be true that someone has a higher IQ. There is no doubt that we do not all have the same level of outer intelligence. The danger comes in when we become proud of it. If we put others down or act superior, then we are spending time thinking of how smart we are compared to others. How can we know the Beloved when we are filled with thoughts of ourselves?

There was a disciple who wanted to visit the home of his Sufi Master. The disciple came to the house and knocked on the door.

The Master asked, "Who is there?"

The disciple said, "It is I." The disciple waited and waited but the Master did not respond. The Master did not invite him in or open the door. The disciple kept knocking, and each time the Master asked who was there, the disciple replied, "It is I." Yet, the Master never opened the door for him.

The disciple left dejected, wondering what was wrong. Along the way, he met another disciple and told him what happened.

"I knocked on the door of the Master's house, and when he asked who was there, I told him it was me. He did not open the door."

The other disciple said, "Let us go back. Let me try and see what happens." The other disciple was a true devotee. His only thoughts were of the Master. He thought about his Master day and night.

When they reached the Master's house, the true disciple knocked on the door.

The Master called from within, "Who is there?"

The true disciple said, "It is you." The Master was overjoyed and opened the door and embraced the disciple, inviting him in.

The first disciple said, "How is it that when I knocked on the door, you did not let me in?"

The Master said, "When I asked who was there, you said it was yourself who was there. The true disciple loses all thoughts of himself and only has thoughts of the Master. To become one with the Beloved, we have to give up all thoughts of duality."

In the lane of love two cannot walk—it is only wide enough for one. When we lose ourselves in the Beloved, the two become one.

We need to rid ourselves of our ego. It means not thinking about how great we are and how insignificant everyone else is. It means thinking of the Beloved. Next time we have thoughts about our own ego, we should ask, "Do we want to think about ourselves, or do we want to let the Beloved into our home?"

A remedy for ego is selfless service. If we spend our time engaged in activities helpful to others, we are serving others instead of ourselves. If we serve without any desire for personal gains, then we are not thinking of ourselves and we are eliminating our ego. We are not thinking of what we can get by doing the work. We are doing service with thoughts of the Beloved. Our hands are busy with work, but our thoughts are to our Beloved. This means that while using our body to do work and get the job done, our thoughts and hearts are engaged in loving the Beloved. We serve with our minds empty of any thoughts of self, but instead think, speak, and act with the Beloved in mind.

If we spend time in service that is selfless, we will not have time to engage in egotistical thoughts.

The Masters provide us with an introspection diary in which each day we can record any lapses in the ethical virtues of nonviolence, truthfulness, purity, humility, and selfless service. The diary also provides a place to note lapses in maintaining the strict vegetarian diet, avoiding all meat, fish, fowl, or eggs, both fertile and infertile, or any by-products of those. There is a place to record failure to avoid all liquor and intoxicating, hallucinogenic, or recreational drugs, as these lower our consciousness, when we are trying to raise our consciousness. How can God enter when we are lowering our consciousness with drugs and alcohol? Thus, vegetarianism and avoidance of drugs and alcohol are prerequisites for initiation into the inner light and sound.

The diary is a tool in which we can evaluate our thoughts, words, and deeds in the areas of nonviolence, truthfulness, humility, purity, and selfless service. When we find a lapse, we can resolve to do better the following day. If we find we have lapsed twenty times in nonviolence of word, we can try to reduce that number the following day to fewer lapses. Then daily we can reduce more and more until we end up with zero lapses in that category. The diary is not meant to chastise ourselves or feel guilty, but to make an honest evaluation of where our thoughts, words, and deeds are focused. Then, we can eliminate lapses until our mind is still, and our soul is clear to meet God within.

Along with noting these lapses in the ethical virtues, the diary also has space to record time spent in meditation in the two practices, meditation on the inner light and meditation on the inner sound, and time spent in selfless service. To also track our spiritual growth, it contains a daily record of what we see and hear within during our meditation. It has places to check off our inner experiences of seeing light of various colors, inner sky, stars, a moon, and a sun, and the radiant form of the Master as our inner guide. It lists the various inner sounds so we can keep a record of what we hear within during meditation on the inner sound. In this way, we keep a daily record of our evolving spiritual progress in meditation on our inner journey back to God.

VISION BLOCKED BY
ATTACHMENT AND DESIRES

The third impediment to clean our inner vision besides our karma and negative thoughts, words, and deeds is that our vision is blocked by all our desires and attachments to things of this world. If you have ever asked your children what they want for their birthdays, they have a long wish list. They want this toy and that toy, this gadget and that gadget, or money to buy whatever else they want. We are no different than our children. Our personal shopping list is filled with all our own wants and desires. We may want material objects such as furniture, electronic equipment, new computers, more clothes, and whatever else is a new fad to keep up with the neighbors. We may desire money, name, or fame. Some may want to become good at a sport or hobby. We may wish to find a certain type of relationship, find a wife or husband, or have children. Some people may want pets. Our heart is filled with numerous desires we want fulfilled. How can we focus on God when we want so many other things in life? To clean our glass to see God, we need to desire God alone. Any other desire that occupies our heart will prevent us from seeing God.

How can we clean our vision if it is blocked with so many desires? To answer this, there is an account from India found in the famous narrative of the Ramayana. Lord Rama went into exile for fourteen years. He stayed in the wilderness. Many yogis lived there doing meditative practices to find God. Also in the forest lived a woman known as a *bhilni*, who in the days of India's caste system was considered to be from a low caste. When she heard Lord Rama was going into exile into the forest, she became elated. She wanted to meet him and thought this would give her a chance to do so.

She thought, "If Lord Rama comes barefooted in this direction, there are so many thorns in the forest they might prick his feet." She began clearing a long pathway, removing all the thorns in case he came that way.

Next, she began thinking, "What if he comes to my hut? What shall I offer him to eat?" She searched for berries growing in the forest. As she did not want him to taste any that were not ripe, she personally tasted them. Those that were sweet, she collected to save for him in her hut.

In the meantime, the other yogis received news of Lord Rama's exile to the jungle. They each thought that because they were all so saintly Lord Rama would visit them. Each was sure Lord Rama would select his hut.

Where did Lord Rama go? He went straight to the hut of the woman who had cleaned the pathway for him and collected the berries. She was beside herself with joy to have her beloved Lord Rama come to her house. She offered him the berries, which he happily ate.

The yogis in the forest were upset. They had been doing penances for many years, yet Lord Rama had not come to their homes. They all came to Lord Rama and asked him to come to visit them.

On the way to their place, there was a pond of water filled with dirt and insects. They said to him, "Lord Rama, we have been living here, but we do not have any fresh water to drink. This lake is so dirty. Could you kindly dip your feet into the lake to purify it for us?"

Lord Rama could read what was in each of their hearts and knew they were each filled with ego. He replied, "You are all yogis. You have been doing penances for so many years. Why don't you put your own feet in the water and cleanse it?" They each put their feet in to clean the lake, but it remained dirty.

"O Lord Rama," they said. "Please put your feet in the lake so it can be cleaned." He wanted to teach them a lesson in love, so he put his feet in and the lake was still not cleaned.

Lord Rama said, "I think that if you want the lake clean, you should call that bhilni—the woman whose home I visited—and ask her to put her feet in the lake."

They were outraged, and thought, "How could

such a low-caste woman be pure enough to clean the lake?" However, since Lord Rama had asked them to do it, they had to obey. They called for the bhilni, and she put her feet in the lake. Suddenly, the lake became clear and clean. Lord Rama had showed these yogis that one whose heart is clear and full of devotion and love radiates that purity everywhere.

The symbolism of this story tells us that if we want God, we need to weed out all imperfections. We need to have a clean place for God. The bhilni wanted to give her Beloved her best. She represents the beauty of the soul within that is reflected without. This story illustrates the power of divine love that cleanses away any impurities.

The result of meditation and ethical living is that our soul becomes like a pure spotless glass, reflecting the light of God. Then, the light burning within us shines its sacred flame of bliss and love to light our pathway to the Divine.

PERSONAL REFLECTION

Spend a week watching your thoughts, words, and deeds. How much time is spent in thoughts, words, or deeds of anger, lust, greed, attachment, and ego? How much of your time and energy is spent in pursuing attachments and desires of this world? Which areas would you like to clear out so you can spend more time thinking about God?

5

VEGETARIAN DIET

When we think about the benefits of a vegetarian diet, we often connect it to the health of our physical body. Doctors and medical researchers describe the benefits a vegetarian diet has for our body. They recommend vegetarianism to reduce illnesses and contribute to our health and wellness. Along with improving our physical well-being, vegetarianism also has benefits for our mind and soul.

Throughout history, many people have adopted a plant-based diet for more than just their physical health. Due to advances in medical science, the effect of diet on our body has only recently been scientifically proven. Without scientific proof, why did people throughout history become vegetarians? Are there other reasons besides the health of the body to be vegetarian?

The universe of vegetarians is populated with spiritually enlightened people. Early Hindu avatars and yogis were vegetarians. Mahavira was a vegetarian. Philosophers, thinkers, writers, civic leaders, and humanitarians throughout history have also adopted the vegetarian diet. Many athletes became vegetarian and gained recognition for their outstanding performance. What did they know about the vegetarian diet that may give us food for thought as well?

There are seven spiritual reasons for vegetarianism:

1: OBSERVING NONVIOLENCE

One spiritual reason for vegetarianism is that it is consistent with leading a life of nonviolence. Many religions teach a common principle—thou shalt not kill. Many founders of various religions, saints, mystics, prophets, gurus, and Masters have taught people not to kill. The Golden Rule implores us to do unto others as we would have others do unto us. Is there anyone who wants to be killed? If we apply the Golden Rule, and we do not want to be killed, then it means that we would not want to kill others.

We need only to look at an animal such as a turkey, cow, or chicken being slaughtered for food; or a fish caught on a fishing hook writhing in pain to realize the suffering they undergo in these violent acts. If we applied the golden rule, we would know for sure we would not want that done to us.

There are those who may think animals, birds, and fish are not conscious. Yet, think of those who own a pet, such as a dog or cat—they treat the animal as if it were a human member of the family. The lower forms of life may not have the faculty to know themselves as people do, but they certainly qualify scientifically under the rubric of living forms—they grow, breathe, eat, and reproduce. They also feel pain. If we are nonviolent, we cannot bear to see any being in pain, whether human or animal. We want to ensure that we are not the inflictors of that pain.

Nonviolence recognizes that all animals and all people are children of God. Those who go within through meditation, explore spiritual realms, and reunite their soul with God see that the light of God shining within us is the same light shining within all life forms. Buddha, Christ, Rama, Krishna, Mahavira, Moses, Guru Nanak, and many other saints and Masters saw the same light in all living beings, including animals. As such, they treated all as one family. For example, St. Francis considered lower forms of life to be our younger brothers and sisters, and he did not want to see animals killed.

The great artist Leonardo da Vinci was a vegetarian who had great compassion. Whenever he saw a caged bird, he paid the owner for the cage and the bird. Then, he would open the cage door and watch the joyful bird soar to freedom.

2: WE ARE WHAT WE EAT

Another spiritual reason for being a vegetarian is to avoid lowering our spiritual consciousness with the vibrations of the animals we ingest. We are what we eat. When we eat an animal, we are making that animal a part of us. We are ingesting not only the body of the animal but also the vibrations of that animal. Some animals have violent tendencies—they are on the prowl for their dinner and attack other animals without compassion. The vibration of that predatory instinct then becomes a part of us.

When we eat animals, not only their vibrations but also their hormones become a part of us. Think of the fear that the animal would be feeling at the end of its life, caged and mistreated, and then on the way to the slaughterhouse. Think of the tremendous fear and panic as the animal is being killed. We know that when we experience fear, the hormones of cortisol and adrenaline are released in our body. They affect us by putting the body in stress and breaking down bodily functions. Those fear hormones remain in the slaughtered animal, and when we eat that animal, they become part of us.

As a prerequisite for initiation into meditation on the light and sound, Masters require a vegetarian diet. Thus, their students do not eat any meat, fish, fowl, or eggs. The Masters teach that God has provided humanity with enough food in the form of plants, so there is no need to take the lives of our younger brothers and sisters in God. They have respect for all forms of life.

3: LOVE FOR ALL

The third spiritual reason that inspired many great religious founders and saints to adopt a vegetarian diet is the principle of love for all. Look at those who realized the Divine. Buddha and Mahavira were full of love and compassion. Guru Nanak Dev Ji Maharaj was all love and compassion. Maulana Rumi was all love and compassion. Jesus was all love and compassion. The Bible teaches, "Love thy neighbor as thyself." Those who taught the principle of having love for all recognized animals as our younger brothers and sisters in God. All religions teach love. This love extends to all life forms, including insects, reptiles, fish, birds, and mammals. To love all includes loving all creation.

Those focused on spirituality, who want to reunite their soul with God, develop love. If we want to love all creation as the great saints and Masters have done, we need to open our hearts to embrace all forms of life, even the lower life forms, in love.

4: SERVICE TO ANIMALS, THE ENVIRONMENT, AND THE PLANET

Another spiritual reason for being vegetarian is to offer selfless service to animals, the environment, and the planet. The word "ecology" involves the root word "oikos," meaning "home." Ecologists regard the whole planet as our home. Just as we do not want to trash our house, pollute our drinking water, suffocate our children with noxious gases, or destroy the resources needed to sustain our house, why would we want to do that to our universal home, the earth?

A vegetarian diet supports care and love for animals and a better use of the earth's resources needed for sustaining humanity today and for posterity. For example, analyses offered by scientists show that the grain needed to feed one cow to be slaughtered for food could be used to feed many times that amount of people. In looking at the earth and a growing population, the vegetarian diet offers a more efficient use of our resources since more people could be fed now and in the future.

Love includes making our planet sustainable today and for posterity. Selfishness is taking from the earth for only ourselves and then destroying it in the process so no one else can reap the same benefits as we have. Greed causes us to take an excessive amount for ourselves, even more than what we need, leaving nothing for others. Greed may be the driving factor that causes people to strip the planet of its resources far beyond their need, leaving nothing for those who do not have even their minimal needs met. Selfishness is using up for ourselves today while not leaving enough for centuries of people in the future. Love is taking steps to care for the planet and its resources and sharing with others today and for posterity.

Spiritual Masters have inspired thousands of people to live with the same regard for the planet and for all forms of life. If we realize the divinity that enlivens all life forms on our planet, we will spread peace and love wherever we go.

5: THE LAW OF KARMA

Another reason saints and founders of various religions promote vegetarianism is that they understand the law of karma. The law of karma can be understood as the ethical application of the third law of physics: for every action there is a reaction.

Science has been investigating the power of vibrations that come from thought. The energy of our brain waves is not limited to remaining inside the skull. Like sound and energy, brain waves can project out from people. Thus, we can pick up the vibrations of others when someone is angry or loving with us. Those vibrations project out from us through our thoughts, words, and deeds, causing reactions. The law of karma states that when any actions are committed, reactions result.

One of the key tenets of religions of the East, such as Hinduism, Buddhism, Sikhism, and Jainism, is that the law of karma affects us at the level of the soul. The law of karma states that all our thoughts, words, and deeds are recorded. Thus, when we have good thoughts, words, or deeds, good has to come back to us. When we have bad thoughts, words, and deeds we must pay the consequences. This is similar to the law of justice in the world, based on a system of punishment and rewards. For example, in the Bible, it is said an "eye for an eye, and a tooth for a tooth." Similarly, some religions believe in judgment in which our deeds in life are judged and that we are placed in the afterlife accordingly.

Saints who explore spiritual realms and realize God bring us their teachings based on their firsthand experiences. Thus, one of the primary reasons for requiring those wanting initiation into the light and sound to become vegetarian is that Masters do not want us to create more karma for ourselves that we would have to pay back. Those who believe in the law of karma believe that if we take the life of an animal, we have to bear the reaction of that action.

Buddhism is filled with many stories of people who did something in a previous life and either had to suffer or had been rewarded for their acts in the same measure in a future existence.

Whether we want to believe in the law of karma or not, it is worth considering that those who have realized God—the saints and mystics—have taught the law of karma based on what they experienced. Those who want to prove the existence of the karmic law to themselves can do what the Masters and saints have done—rise above this physical consciousness, explore the inner spiritual realms, and reunite their soul with the Creator. By doing so, the clarity of the laws of creation will be known and one can then act accordingly.

Those who have had near-death experiences have described that when they entered regions of light, they had a life review. They saw all the good and bad they had done. Not only did they witness it, but they actually experienced what the other people felt when they did good or harm to others. This experience was so profound that they realized that the most important principle was that of love. In fact, they came back from the NDE transformed by the light. They felt compelled to lead their lives in a more loving, caring manner since they had experienced the reaction of the harm they had caused people and the reaction of the joy they brought to others.

6: BENEFITS TO MEDITATION

One of the spiritual reasons to be vegetarian is to boost one's meditation. In meditation, if we wish to experience ourselves as soul, rise above physical consciousness to explore spiritual realms within, and ultimately reunite the soul with God, a vegetarian diet speeds our progress. To enter realms of light and love, we need to develop ethical virtues. We need to have the purity of heart by which we can experience the Creator. We want to lighten our load of karma and not add to it.

By following a vegetarian diet, we develop nonviolence, love, and service to other forms of life. If we lead a life of nonviolence and love, we purify our soul to enter ethereal realms within and reunite our soul with the Oversoul.

When the Bible says, "Thou shalt not kill," there is no rider in its meaning saying that it only refers to people. It refers to not killing—period. That means not killing animals either. Buddhism, Jainism, and Hinduism also have nonviolence as a basic tenet of leading a spiritual life.

Masters have said that God is love and the way back to God is through love. They teach that when we are loving to all people and all forms of life, we are on the way back to God. Those who have been successful on the spiritual path know that vegetarianism aids meditation and spiritual progress.

7: SPIRITUAL ENLIGHTENMENT

The seventh spiritual reason for being a vegetarian is to attain spiritual enlightenment. Spiritual Masters have required a vegetarian diet as a prerequisite for initiation to learn meditation on the inner light and sound. Why? The Master gives a special dispensation at initiation in which our past karmas are burned away. Only those karmas left for this life remain. For spiritual progress, we want to make sure we do not accumulate new karmas. At initiation, what was done in the past—our sanchit or storehouse karmas—are eliminated. From this point forward, we also do not want to add to our karmic load. That would be like trying to wash clothes in a washing machine, but as the clean water washes away the grime, we keep adding more dirty water.

Killing and eating animals add new karmas. Masters teach that to gain spiritual enlightenment and oneness with the Creator, we need to reduce our karmas. Thus, we do not want to live on a diet that takes the life of any animals. This is the reason that vegetarianism is required for initiation into the inner light and sound.

These are seven spiritual secrets of the vegetarian diet. The benefits of the vegetarian diet are that it is good for our body and mind, and most importantly, good for our soul. Vegetarianism can aid our spiritual progress if we want to know our true selves as soul, explore spiritual realms within, and experience reunion with God.

PERSONAL REFLECTION

List what you eat in your current diet, and see how many ways you can eliminate meat, fish, fowl, or eggs by switching them to plant-based food choices (fruits, vegetables, nuts, seeds, legumes, beans, grains, and milk products unless you choose to be vegan). Visit a health food section of a food store, or restaurants that serve vegetarian dishes to see the variety of substitutes there are for the flesh of animals. Try vegetarian foods and track differences in how you feel physically, mentally, and spiritually.

6

SELFLESS SERVICE

The spiritual progress we make through meditation, ethical living, a vegetarian diet, and the love and grace of a spiritual Master is further accelerated through engaging in selfless service.

Selfless service opens our heart to love and help others. It makes us an instrument of God's love by providing for all of God's creation, whether other people, animals, or the planet. In serving, we develop qualities of being giving, caring, and loving. Serving selflessly helps to eliminate our ego and our selfishness.

The following story illustrates the value of self-lessness. A wealthy person was working with his lawyer in preparing his will. The lawyer was impressed with both the amount of money the man had accumulated and the number of servants he had. The man had many people to attend to his every need, including drivers, butlers, house cleaners, and gardeners to tend to his estate. The man was proud of how many people he employed to serve him. He felt it was a sign of his success in life.

When the man finally passed on, he waited for his judgment. He felt he would receive a good placement in heaven because he had been so successful in life.

When his turn came to be judged, the angel looked over his records and reflected on what he had accomplished in life.

After looking through the entire record of this man, she declared that he did not merit time in heaven.

"What do you mean?" the man exclaimed. "Didn't you see how successful I was and how many people served me?"

The angel replied, "For entry into heaven, we do not keep records of how many people served you. For entry into heaven, we only record how many people you served. Unfortunately, your entry into heaven is denied, because in your life, you only served yourself."

This story illustrates a powerful lesson. Many people focus on amassing their own empires and estates, thinking this is the true purpose in life. Yet, they disregard the purpose for which God made humanity. True human beings live for others. Some scriptures say that if God wanted only devotion, the angels were there for that purpose. God wanted to create beings that would serve others, and thus God created humans. It is clear from the story that service to others rather than service to ourselves paves the way for our return to God.

Consider which people from history humanity best remembers. Are they the people who had others serve them, or are they the ones who served others? If we scan the pages of history, we find we do not remember or honor the emperors and kings who lived during the time of Jesus Christ. Such kings may have had large numbers of slaves and servants catering to them, yet we remember Jesus Christ because he was one who served others. His life was one of sacrifice and service to the suffering souls of his time.

We do not honor the ruthless rulers who used many a servant to meet their needs as well as to conquer and subjugate others. Rather, we remember the nonviolent Buddha whose life was one of service to others by helping them achieve an end to suffering.

If we think of the number of wealthy people who have lived over the centuries, their names may have been obliterated by the sands of time; while the names of those noble people who spent their lives as scientists, explorers, humanitarian leaders, great teachers, and heroes to help make other people's lives better are etched permanently in history.

Into which category do we wish to fall when our life is reviewed at its end? Do we wish to go into the spiritual realms after this life ends with an empty list of those we served because we were more concerned with having other people serve us?

If we examine the lives of the great saints and Masters, we find they were imbued with humility. Rather than having people serve them, they considered themselves the servants of the people. There were countless people who recalled how saints and Masters had personally served them and made their lives better.

Saints and Masters serve selflessly, making the spiritual and mundane lives of others easier. If each person who met a Master recorded the numerous ways the Master humbly served him or her, it might take decades to read all those accounts. Masters consider themselves to be servants of God and servants of the children of God. That is their role on earth. They come to serve humanity, not to have humanity serve them. They roam the earth in search for souls to serve. They serve others spiritually, by reconnecting their souls to God. Along with that, out of compassion, they help disciples with their mundane lives and do whatever it takes to turn their attention to God. Masters help people with their physical and emotional problems, their relationship issues, their family struggles, their careers, their financial burdens, and many other difficulties. At the time of initiation, the Masters perform the highest service by taking over the karmic accounts of the disciples, and at times, out of compassion, they even take on the karmic suffering of a disciple on their own bodies. There are countless ways in which Masters are servants to the family of God.

There are several columns on the Sant Mat introspection diary for selfless service, both physical and financial. One column is provided to record time spent in selfless service. The other column is for noting any lapses in selfless service, either physical or financial. That means that if a chance to serve selflessly or help someone is not taken, it is noted as a lapse or a missed opportunity. In this way, we can observe our attitude towards service and resolve to be of more help to others on each successive day.

There are numerous ways we can be of service to others. Life is filled with many service opportunities. Selfless service ennobles us and makes us fit to enter the realm of God.

We can help people physically. Those who are ill can be helped in many ways. If they are unable to take care of themselves, we can get them food and medicine. We can help transport them for their medical care. We can perform chores for people who are unable to do such things for themselves due to illness.

Some people need help intellectually. We can teach others to improve in a skill. We can listen to their difficulties and help them find solutions for their concerns.

Some people need financial help. While we do not want to give money to people who will misuse it for harmful activities, we can evaluate whether they truly will benefit from monetary assistance. We can help victims of various natural disasters, by providing shelter, clothing, or medicine to people in devastated areas. We can donate to places that help people spiritually or physically. Many religions encourage people to donate a portion of their income as selfless service, and the Masters have always recommended tithing regularly.

Spiritual service is offered by Masters, who give their charged attention as a catalyst to help us reconnect with the Divine. The Master offers us initiation into a meditation technique that connects us to the light and sound current upon which we can journey back to God. Masters also take over our karmic accounts, so our burden is lightened and we can rise above the three lower realms to enter spiritual realms beyond. They teach people how to meditate so they can discover their true self as soul and reunite with God in this lifetime.

There is another profound benefit to selfless service. Selfless service, or seva, provides an opportunity to engage in good works without creating karma. Lord Krishna has pointed out that all thoughts, words, and deeds create karma, either good or bad. Good karma creates chains of gold, while bad karma creates chains of iron. They are both chains that bind us to the world. There is nothing wrong with doing good, but we need to do so in a way that does not bind us further to the world and cause us to create more karma. Good karma brings us back to the world to reap rewards and prevents us from escaping the three lower regions to reunite with God.

When people have a desire to do good, how can they do so without creating karma? The way to do this is to do the service in the name of God without desiring any reward for ourselves. When we do something for someone else but expect a reward, then it creates karma. If we do good without expecting a reward, then we are not creating karma. Also, if we do it because it is God's work and we just want to be helping hands to God, then there is no karma attached.

Another aspect of selfless service is making sure that we do not accumulate karma while doing the service by becoming caught up in the five thieves of anger, lust, greed, attachment, and ego. If while doing seva, we get angry, then we are not being selfless and we are creating karma for ourselves. If while doing seva we are filled with attachment and ego, then we are not being selfless and are creating karma for ourselves. This means that we have to do seva with a pure mind and a pure heart. We need to be nonviolent, truthful, pure, humble, loving, and detached while doing selfless service.

Sometimes when there is seva to be done, we want to pick and choose which type to do. This is another example of ego getting in the way of serving selflessly. Some people feel they only want to do seva that brings them prestige, name, fame, or other personal gain. Such people refuse service that needs to be done if they consider it beneath them. Doing selfless service means doing what is needed, and not considering ourselves too high and mighty for certain types of service.

In this connection, there is an anecdote from history. An army of soldiers was on the battlefield trying to lift a large piece of timber to use as a battering ram to knock down the wall of a fortress. A corporal stood by the side commanding the men to heave harder to lift the timber. A stranger rode by on his horse and observed the scene.

He said to the corporal, "Don't you think if you helped them, the strength of one more man may help lift the timber? Why don't you help them?"

The corporal replied, "That is not my job. I am the corporal. It is for them to do that work. That is not the work of a corporal!"

With that, the stranger dismounted from his horse, joined the ranks of the soldiers and helped them to lift the timber. The added strength of one man was all it took to lift the wood. Having completed the task, the stranger mounted his horse.

Before departing, the stranger turned to the corporal and said, "The next time you have a piece of timber you need help lifting, corporal, call for the commander in chief."

It was then that the men realized that the stranger was none other than George Washington, the commander in chief of the army, who would become the first president of the United States.

All types of service have a purpose and should be considered equally important. If we truly want to develop a spirit of selfless service, we must feel that no job is too high and no job is too low or beneath us. All jobs are important. Whether we are preparing food or cleaning up after eating, both jobs are equal in the eyes of God, when performed selflessly. Whether we are typing, making photocopies, gardening, or throwing out the trash, they all have equal benefit as service. Whenever we refuse a type of seva with the attitude that certain work is beneath us, then we are serving with our ego and the benefit we receive by being selfless is lost. We should serve in whatever way is needed with love and humility for that will give us the true benefit of doing seva.

If we serve with an attitude that a particular seva makes us more important than others, then we are not serving selflessly but are using seva as an opportunity to make a name for ourselves.

If we do seva because we hope we will receive some financial or material gain, then that also is not selfless.

If we do seva because we want power to control

others and boss them around, then that is not selfless. Instead, we are creating karma for ourselves by wanting power and position. Wanting to control others leads to us getting angry when others do not do what we want. Then, we add more karma by being angry. If we are trying to manipulate others and have to deceive and lie to do so, then we are creating karma while doing the service and that also is not selfless.

The proper attitude towards seva is that it is an opportunity to do good without creating karma that will bind us to the world. It is an opportunity to serve with our focus on God.

Masters speak of the benefits of seva as being no less than the benefits received from meditation. Seva cannot take the place of meditation, but it aids meditation. When we perform service selflessly in the name of God, with our attention fixed on God and we mentally repeat the five charged Words, when we later meditate, we will derive the same benefit from the seva as if we had been meditating during that time. This will provide a great spiritual boost for our meditation. Wanting a spiritual boost in our meditation is not selfish, nor does it mean we want a reward. When we do seva to remember God and help our soul, that kind of reward does not create any karma. We do selfless service because it is a chance to help God's creation. Selfless service expands our soul and helps us develop spiritually.

If we serve with the right attitude, we will not create new karma and we will stay focused on God. When we meditate, we will reap the fruits of having done seva. We will find that day by day, our spiritual progress will increase.

Let us live our lives serving others. We will find that we will be imbued with the joy and grace of giving selflessly, and that our souls will be purified and reunited with God.

PERSONAL REFLECTION

Add to your schedule some selfless service activities. Observe your attitude and consider if you can do service without desiring any material reward, name, fame, power, or financial gain. See if you can serve without wanting any reward for yourself. Note how such selfless service makes you feel.

7

SPIRITUAL UPLIFTMENT

When a fire is first lit, the flame needs protection from being extinguished. Similarly, we need to tend the spark of light illumining our soul. A spiritual Master provides a protective shield around our spark to maintain it through a spiritual gathering called satsang. "Satsang" literally means "communion with truth." It is a gathering in which we can discover who we are as soul, whether there is God, and how to meditate to experience these truths firsthand.

BENEFITS OF SATSANG

Some may ask, "What is the purpose of getting together at a weekly satsang? Why should we travel from our homes to a weekly satsang gathering?" These questions may seem reasonable if satsang is considered to be a lecture given by any speaker or a place to hear talks that can be read for ourselves in a book. Satsang is more than the oral content of the program. Satsang has a spiritual charging, the subtle effect of which can elevate us spiritually. It protects us from the influences of the worldly distractions that slow our spiritual progress.

It helps us maintain our spiritual flame.

What are the benefits of attending satsang? People are searching for answers to the mysteries of life and death. They want to discover if there is really God, if there is a soul, if there is life after death, and what will happen to us when this life ends. These basic questions lead one to explore spirituality.

Spirituality is not only an intellectual study. Intellectual answers to questions about the mystery of life and death are not satisfying because one may still have doubts about whether or not they are true or not. One wonders if those who wrote or orally gave answers to these spiritual questions through the ages were right. The only answer that satisfies those who want proof is personal experience. Only when we can see for ourselves the truth of what was written in the scriptures or described orally by saints over centuries do we truly believe and have faith.

Spirituality is proven by firsthand experience. To attain this proof, we need to do more than read books and listen to lectures. We need to perform practices to experience inner spiritual truths. The process leads from this outer world to the inner world. It is a step-by-step scientific experiment. A Master teaches those steps so we can see for ourselves the inner proof of a spiritual existence.

It is not easy to find God. It is a process of withdrawing our attention from the world outside to focus within. Many worldly attractions draw our attention outward. It takes tremendous strength to resist outer diversions that keep our attention from meditation so we can know God, know our soul, and connect the two. To keep our attention spiritually focused, saints offer the gift of satsang.

Satsang offers protection to keep the flame burning. A hectic life leaves little time for spiritual practices. We need to find time in our daily routines for meditation.

Satsang provides a sacred space in which we can close the door to the world for an hour or two to focus on our soul and God. In a satsang meeting, people can meditate together. There are no distractions because all are meditating. The rest of the time in satsang is spent listening to spiritual discourses to remind us of our true purpose of life. The discourses, meditation, and spiritual charging of the satsang refocus our mind on the importance of meditation, ethical living, the vegetarian diet, selfless service, and attaining communion of our soul with God. It motivates us to put in time for meditation through the rest of the week. It recommends us to engage in spiritual practices on a daily basis.

Satsang awakens us to activities that are truly helpful. If we engage all week in worldly pursuits, satsang draws our attention to the spiritual side of life. Satsang is a wakeup call to people of all ages to spend some time daily communing with God within.

SPIRITUAL CHARGING

Another benefit of going to satsang is the spiritual upliftment we receive through the grace of a Master. The attention of a saint carries a spiritual charging. When a saint puts his attention on us, our soul experiences upliftment. Although our outer senses may be oblivious to what is happening, our soul recognizes a boost from a spiritual energy source. The more receptive we are, the more aware we are of this upliftment. Whether we realize it physically or not, the Master's spiritually charged attention is bestowed on everyone in the satsang arena. All those who attend receive a spiritual benefit. Those who are receptive feel the charged atmosphere upon entering. They receive a boost that helps their meditations, both during satsang or when they meditate anywhere else throughout the week. Seekers who attend satsang to learn more about spirituality also receive benefits, such as feeling peaceful and calm, experiencing a spiritual stirring, or undergoing an awakening to their need to find God. Some report having spiritual inner experiences at a satsang.

That charging does not only remain with us for the duration of satsang; it can stay with us throughout the week. While attending to our worldly work and responsibilities the rest of the week, a spiritual undercurrent can flow within us. We feel spiritually connected. The problems of the world do not bother us as much. We can focus better when we sit for meditation. By attending satsang, even our loved ones may notice a change in us when we start acting in a calmer, more spiritual, and more loving manner.

There is tremendous grace bestowed on us in the company of a saint. We have no idea of the amount of grace being afforded to us by a spiritual Master, both in his physical presence and through his attention poured on us in satsang.

In satsang, the Master shows us the pitfalls and obstacles in the way. He helps us steer clear of them so we can complete the journey successfully and in the shortest possible time. After all, we have only a limited number of years to make the journey. Much of our life has already passed. We have to proceed as quickly as we can in the time we have left. Trial and error can take time. Isn't it better to use a tried and true method that will give us the results we want?

At satsang, we are reminded of the spiritual treasures within us and how to make the best use of initiation into the inner light and sound. If we look for spiritual gifts in the outer world, our mind will remain in doubt. It is only when we go within that we can remove all doubts and see for ourselves that we are soul and there is God. The Master at the time of initiation puts us in touch with the light and sound within so we can reunite with God. We can then see the light of God and hear the divine Song. This Song has been called Word in the Bible, Naad or Jyoti and Sruti in the Hindu scriptures, Sraosha in the Zoroastrian scriptures, Sonorous Light in the Buddhist scriptures, Naam or Shabd by the Sikhs, Voice of Silence by Theosophists and many other terms in different languages. It is the power of God manifesting in creation. This experience of inner light and sound is unlike anything in this physical world. It is not like reading a book or getting an educational degree. It is beyond the realm of intellectual knowledge. It is an experience filled with intoxicating bliss, divine rapture, tremendous light beyond any we could see in this world, and music so uplifting that no worldly music compares to it. Satsang reinforces the importance of meditation to find these treasures of inner light and sound.

SATSANG IS OPEN TO ALL

We are all children of one God. The light and sound current is available to all. That is why the satsang of a Master teaching meditation on the inner light and sound is open to people of all religions, nationalities, cultures, ages, and walks of life. God wants all to return Home. Just as a mother feeds all her children, God has made the gift of the light and sound available to all who seek it. God does not discriminate between people of different religions or even those who are agnostic or atheists. God does not care if our skin color is dark or light, or whether our eyes are blue, brown, green, or black. God does not care if we are rich or poor, literate or illiterate. God provides a way for all to return Home. A satsang is a protective place in which people from all faiths can enter and commune with God within their own selves. The wine of God's love is for the whole world. Saints and Masters have come to pour out without end so that the whole world may drink. Masters lovingly give the nectar of the light and sound to all who are thirsty.

God has entrusted the saints with the task of bringing the lost children back Home. The saints walk the earth in search of souls crying to return to God. Many people have the idea that the saints come to take back only saintly people. There is a false idea that one must already be holy and perfect to come to the satsang of a saint. However, if we look back through history we find that every saint came to help anyone crying for the Lord, whether a pious person or a sinner.

There is a story from the life of Lord Krishna. One day, Lord Krishna was invited by a rich person to attend a feast. The rich person set up a beautiful table, lavishly decorated with fine plates and utensils. Many special elaborately prepared foods were laid before Lord Krishna. As Lord Krishna looked at the table, he noticed there was one cup on the table that had a defect in it.

He requested of the host, "I would like to eat out of that cup first."

The rich man, noticing the cup's blemish, said, "Oh, no, my dear One, do not use that cup. It is broken. Use this fine cup instead."

But Lord Krishna insisted he wanted to eat from the defective cup. He pulled the cup in front of him and put the food in it. Then he began to eat.

The rich man fell at Lord Krishna's feet, moved by this gesture, and said, "O Lord, do you deal with people as you have done with the cup, by choosing the broken vessel first?"

The rich man felt that if there was hope for a broken cup, there must also be hope for him.

This story illustrates the fact that the saints come for all, including the broken, downhearted, and imperfect souls yearning for the Lord. Their job is to take separated souls back to God. Once a soul is truly yearning for the Lord, the saints and Masters find them to take them Home. Sant Kirpal Singh Ji Maharaj beautifully said, "Every saint has a past, and every sinner a future." The compassion of the saints is to open their satsangs to all those who want to return to God even if they had been living the life of a sinner.

Look at the compassion that Christ took upon a prostitute. When people wanted to stone her for her sins, Jesus said, "Let those of you who are without sin throw the first stone." When he said that, no one else dared throw a stone because they all knew that they were not free of sin.

The job of the Master is to clean us up to get us ready to go Home. Doctors are not there for healthy people; they open their clinics to those who are ill. Their job is to make the ill become healthy. Teachers are not there for those who already have a doctorate degree. They open their classrooms for those who need to be taught. Their job is to teach those who want to learn. Similarly, saints are not here for the perfect ones. They come for the imperfect to make them godly.

Some people are filled with guilt thinking they are not worthy of receiving the spiritual teachings. But we are all in the same boat. Masters open their satsangs to all who have a sincere cry in their heart to know God. Rather than dwell on thoughts that we are not worthy or that we are not capable of spiritual progress, we should realize that the Masters are compassionate. Our job is to forget the past and do no more. The Masters teach the worthy and unworthy alike how to return to God.

We should not worry if we are like the broken cup. The Masters are moved by compassion when they see our broken vessels. They want to answer our cries and make our vessels whole. We should be grateful to the Masters for their grace in taking even those with failings under their wings. Once we enter the arena of a Master's satsang, we are in the hands of the Master and our progress back Home will surely take place. It is our choice whether we will speed up our progress by following the steps given by the Master at satsang or slow it down by ignoring those steps. Satsang gives us both a spiritual boost to uplift our meditations and right understanding of the steps to reunite our soul with God. These steps include meditation, ethical living, a vegetarian diet, selfless service, and attending satsang.

One of the great developments towards embracing people of all religions was the custom of *langar* or free kitchen before or after satsang. This practice was established by the fifth Sikh Guru, Guru Arjan Dev Ji Maharaj. Hundreds of years ago he instituted a free kitchen or langar in which people of all religions, economic backgrounds, castes, and walks of life could eat together side by side. Previously, people were conscious of religious and caste differences, and people from different levels of society would not eat with those of other groups. The saints saw the oneness within each and demonstrated this by setting the example of joining people together for meals as one family under God. Satsang offers the same benefit of bringing people together to pray and meditate together as children of one God.

A HEDGE AROUND THE SAPLINGS

When one plants a young tree, the sapling is in danger of the forces of nature that may knock it down. To protect the sapling, one puts a small hedge around it. Besides meditation and ethical living, satsang also offers a protective hedge that helps our tree of spirituality to grow. When new to the spiritual teachings it is easy to become diverted from our goal by the many temptations that bombard us. Satsang provides a protective hedge to remind us to meditate. It focuses us on leading an ethical life. It helps us stay on the vegetarian diet. It gives us a chance to cleanse and purify ourselves through selfless service. At satsang, we also find that our questions are answered. Unanswered questions rankle in our mind and can take us into a tailspin. Satsang is a place in which we can find answers and deepen our understanding of the spiritual teachings. Satsang puts us in touch with like-minded people who want to know God. By keeping company of people who want to meditate and find God, we are strengthened. Our growing tree receives at satsang the nourishment of the charging and blessings of the saint. It fills us from our roots to our branches with love, grace, and spiritual upliftment.

Satsang is the protective shelter of a fire pit that protects the flames from being exposed to the heavy rains and winds of a passing storm. The charging of the satsang helps to speed our progress on the spiritual way so we can attain our goal of the soul's union with God.

PERSONAL REFLECTION

*If possible, attend a spiritual gathering or satsang,
or a get together with others who have a like-minded
interest in spirituality. Note any difference in your focus
on spirituality after attending such a gathering.*

PART
THREE

8

RECEPTIVITY

OUR SPARK IS LIT BY A spiritual Master at the time of initiation into the inner light and sound. Next, we maintain the flame when we learn to meditate, lead an ethical living, become a vegetarian and avoid alcohol and intoxicating or hallucinogenic drugs, perform selfless service, and attending satsang. Finally, we merge our individual spark into the dazzling Eternal Flame illuminating our soul and spreading light to the whole world. We can reach this ultimate stage when we further ignite our spark by developing receptivity, a ruling passion, gratitude, and love.

Receptivity is an openness to receive the light, love, and bliss of the Eternal Flame. It involves keeping our floodgates open to receive all the treasures of the Divine.

Two analogies help us understand the state of receptivity.

One is the image of the empty cup, and the other is the image of a computer downloading information.

THE EMPTY CUP

Being receptive is like being an empty cup. This describes the attitude we should adopt in meditation and in our spiritual life. In meditation, pitchers of divine wine of spiritual love cascade into us from God. If we meditate like an empty cup, we can receive perpetually of the wine of ecstasy.

Meditation should be an effortless effort. We close our eyes and simply gaze at what lies in front of us, without any thought of what will or should appear. The sooner we sit in that state, the sooner we will have inner progress. It is for God to decide what to give us within. For example, sometimes when meditating, we get distracted by thoughts such as wanting to see a particular colored light or inner experience. Our mind becomes so determined to see what it wants to see that it distracts us from our concentration. In meditation, we should not be disturbed by thoughts generated from our mind. Even sitting with a preconceived idea of what we should see is considered a distraction of thought. If our mind is constantly thinking of what it wants to receive in meditation, it is blocking the way for the divine grace to enter. It is like a friend is knocking at our door, but he or she cannot enter because we are standing in the doorway. The very thought of what we expect to see in our meditation is an obstacle for it keeps our mind active and we cannot focus our attention on the inner light. We merely have to sit at the door and wait. God will fill us with more grace and blessings than we could ever have dreamed of. If we sit in humility and keep our hearts open for whatever God wants to give us, pitchers upon pitchers of the sweet waters of life will pour into us. The divine wine of the light and sound will flow through us and around us, and we will be satiated with bliss and inebriated with the wine of spiritual love.

The poet-saint Sant Darshan Singh Ji Maharaj said in a verse:

> Who is the ecstasy-producing Cupbearer
> who has stepped among us today?
> He pours out cup after cup of the Elixir of the Word
> so that all may drink his fill.

The Cupbearer is a poetic term for a spiritual Master who serves the divine wine of God. The Cupbearer is circulating through the universe ready to pour out the elixir of life. God will pour it through any open conduit. Those who meditate and are open to receive God's gift will surely receive it. Those who are wrapped up in their own thoughts close themselves off from receiving God's bountiful blessings. Yet, God never gives up. God continues sending divine grace in the hopes that each person will turn his or her attention within to receive it. God is continuously pouring out love and spiritual blessings. We merely have to turn our cup upright to catch them.

Becoming like an empty cup is a way of life. It extends beyond meditation into our everyday living. A Master-disciple relationship is based on firsthand experience. When we first come to a Master, we see how a Master is all goodness, sweetness, kindness, and affection. Through continued contact, we also see that everything the Master teaches is proved by our own experiences on the spiritual path. At initiation, the Master gives us a capital with which to start in the form of inner proof that there is something beyond this physical world. That initial capital is contact with the inner light and sound. With daily meditation, that inner experience increases, and we find that the theoretical aspect of the spiritual teachings is proven by firsthand practical experience. This motivates us to continue the practice to perfect the meditation so we can rise beyond this physical realm to experience inner spiritual realms. With each added experience, we realize more and more that what the Master is saying is borne out by inner proof. That is why Masters say not to believe what the Master is saying until one sees and proves it for oneself. Meditation gives the experimental process by which we can prove that the inner experiences of light and sound, the inner spiritual realms, the soul, and God are verifiable.

Little by little, we find out that the Master is our best friend, teacher, and guide. The Master wants only the best for us. He takes care of us in all spheres of life. While others in life may cause us pain, the Master heals all sufferings and pains. We begin to realize that the Master is our true benefactor and we develop trust and faith in him.

Once this trust and faith is established, we gain confidence in what the Master teaches. Thus, we start engaging in the spiritual practices more closely. We know that whatever guidance is given by the Master will surely help us because we are proving what is being taught by firsthand experience through meditation.

Meditation with the attitude that we are an empty cup is the highest state of prayer. It means that we do not even ask for anything but just wait lovingly and devotedly for whatever God wants to give. It is a prayer in which we know that God will give us what is best for us.

In this connection there is a story about a man who prayed to God, saying, "God, please speak to me." While praying, a bird on a tree began chirping and singing. Yet, the man did not listen to it.

The man continued to pray, saying, "God speak to me." Suddenly, thunder boomed and lightning flashed in the sky. But the man did not notice it.

That night, the man sat again for prayer and said, "God, let me see you!" A star shone brightly in the sky. Yet the man did not see it.

The man became impatient, and shouted, "God, show me a miracle." At that moment, a baby was born to a neighbor and let out its first cry of life. But the man did not notice it. The next day, the man went outside.

While walking, the man silently prayed to God,

"God, touch me and let me know that you are here with me." Suddenly, a butterfly landed on the man's arm. But the man brushed it away.

The man finally cried, "God, I need your help." The man received a letter from a friend telling him how he discovered a way to find God, but the man tore up the letter and threw it out. The man was in despair, and cried and cried, making one last request to God to communicate with him.

Finally, God appeared to the man in a vision and said, "Do not fear, my son, you are loved. But you are missing out on my blessings because they do not appear in the form that you expect them!"

This story describes our condition. We pray to God, but because we want the blessings to come in the way we want, we miss out on the blessings that God sends. We include an instruction manual with our prayer telling God how we want the blessings to come. When they do not come in the way we want, we disregard the fact that God sent us our blessing. If we look back on the blessing later in life, we realize that what God sent us was far better than what we had imagined or asked for. Sometimes, we ask for something that is not really good for us, or not as good as what God actually wants to give us. Let us instead learn to be receptive to what God sends us. If we are patient and wait, we will receive far more than what we had asked for. We will find that God will give us greater gifts than what we could ever dream of. If we are patient and calm we will realize that God knows what is best.

Acceptance does not come easily. At first we begin by praying for one thing or another. Praying for something in particular has its pitfalls. Sometimes we may have our prayer answered right away, and other times not at all. If we do not get what we want, there is the danger of our becoming disappointed, disillusioned, and depressed. We lose faith and feel that God has not listened to us and is not responding. But when we do not pray for anything other than what God wants to give, there is no danger of disappointment. It takes time to develop to a point where we can pray in this manner. The faith and trust in God must first develop. That is born out of our experiences. Once that develops, then we relax and put ourselves into God's care. We have the confidence that God will act as our friend, benefactor, and protector.

"Sweet is Thy will" is the highest state of receptivity. It is a condition in which our mind is stilled and our ego is at rest. It is best described by a formula: humans minus the mind equals God. In this condition, nothing stands between God and us. We become an empty cup, and the pure waters of divinity can flow unhampered into us. There are no distractions, no separation, and no duality. The Power of God permeates our entire being. In this state, we merge back in God.

To derive the greatest benefit from the blessings bestowed by God, we should adopt this humble attitude of the empty vessel. Our mind will be emptied of its ceaseless desires and distractions. We will instead be open to receive wave after wave, pitcher after pitcher, of sweet grace. We will find ourselves attaining union with God in the shortest possible time.

DOWNLOADING GOD

We can also compare receptivity to the way a computer downloads information. Receptivity is a state in which we download God into ourselves. Unfortunately, instead of downloading God, we are downloading the world into ourselves. How can we download God instead of the world to reap more spiritual benefits?

Think about how a computer works. A computer starts out as basic hardware. On its own it can do nothing. To operate, software programs have to be downloaded to it. These software programs carry out different tasks and functions. Although all computers are basically the same, they operate differently based on the software downloaded into it.

Human beings are like computer hardware. We are all born with the same basic operating equipment. We have a physical body, bodily systems, and the brain with its system of taking information from the body and senses. What makes us different is the kind of input that is downloading into our self over the course of our lives. We all download different types of input from the world. Most people only download information into themselves that comes from their body, their senses, and the outer world.

Receptivity is downloading software from God

instead of from programs of this world. The soul is not interested in downloading the world with its enjoyments and entertainments. It wants to download the Divine and its bliss, love, and ecstasy.

To illustrate this, there is a story about a disciple who went to a spiritual Master and asked to find out who was the best devotee of God. This disciple thought he was the most devoted and was surprised to find out that there was one more devoted than he was.

The Master said, "Here is a location for you to go. You will find someone more devoted than you." The disciple was given directions and set off to find this great devotee.

When the disciple reached the location, he thought he was lost or had been given wrong directions. There was no house. There was no building. There were no streets. It was a spot in nature surrounded by trees and a lake. He thought he was sent on a wild goose chase because there were no human beings there.

He looked around and all he saw was a bird sitting on a tree branch. He kept looking but no person appeared. It was just the man and the bird.

Being tired from the trip he sat down under the shade of the tree. As he sat there he took a closer look at the bird. He noticed the bird was totally starving and parched. The bird was frail and looked like he would keel over and die at any moment.

Feeling sorry for the bird, he wanted to give the bird some water from the lake below it.

The man thought, "This is strange. Here is a bird dying of thirst, yet a few feet away is the water from a clean lake."

The man took a cupful of water from the lake into his hands and held it out to the bird. The bird did not fly down to drink the water even from his cupped hands.

Finally, the man spoke aloud his thoughts, saying, "Hey bird, what is the problem? You are dying of thirst and here is a lake a few feet away. Why don't you drink from it?"

The man was surprised to hear the bird answer.

The bird said, "Thank you, but I do not drink that kind of water. I only drink the purest rain drops from the heavens. That is all I want. If I do not get it I am not settling for any substitute water like this lake water. That will not satisfy me. I will wait as I am only satiated with the pure rain water from above."

The man then realized why this bird was the most devoted of all. It was focused on only one thing—the purest rainwater. It would wait and only accept that water for its fulfillment.

This bird symbolizes our soul. Our soul is only fulfilled by union with God. It is not satisfied by anything of this world.

If we identify with our true self, the soul, the computer operator of our body and brain, we too will find that downloading this world does not fulfill us. The soul is only nourished by the love and light of the Divine.

To be truly fulfilled, we need to download God. How can we do that? Meditation is the process of downloading God. When we meditate, our soul comes in contact with the vibrating principle of God, the current of light and sound. The point of connection is at the third or single eye, between and behind the two eyebrows. When we put our attention there, we begin the download process in which we connect with the light and sound of God. When that is complete, we are then connected to the entire network of God. We merge into the light and sound and can travel on the current through all the realms of creation, transcending realms of matter to enter realms of spirit. The ultimate end of the journey is merging back into God, an infinite ocean of consciousness and love.

When we download God into our system, we are actually merging our real nature back into our Source. We then tap into eternal wisdom, immortality, bliss, happiness, peace, and divine love. We transcend this world of pain and suffering to enter a realm with no death, no pain, and no suffering. We experience an ecstasy and love unknown to us in this physical world.

Meditation is a time to download God. However, what do most of us do in meditation? After stilling our body, instead of also stilling the mind, we continue downloading the world. This is where the problem begins. We are thinking during our meditation time. We are downloading our past. We are downloading our wishes for the future. We are downloading our thoughts of anger, lust, greed, attachment, and ego. We are downloading the desires of our senses. Receptivity is downloading God in our meditation.

To download God, we need to keep our mind still. The spiritual Master is a master programmer who can make the connection between us and the light and sound. Initiation is like a computer expert connecting our computer to the programs we need. The Master can help us download God by teaching us the meditation technique on the inner light and sound. That is why Masters at initiation give five Words to repeat that are spiritually charged by their attention. The meditation practice, called simran, or silent repetition of these Words, has a special function. Repetition of these Words jumpstarts our attention to withdraw from the operating system of the body and mind to rise to a point where we can download the current of light and sound. The light and sound current connects us to the source of all love, wisdom, and bliss.

When we are paying attention to our thoughts during meditation, we are downloading the world. When we are not thinking, but keeping our mind still, we are able to download God. The repetition of the Words spiritually charged by a Master keeps our mind from intervening. Then, we can be open and receptive to receive the light and sound within us.

When we meditate and are distracted by thoughts, we can stop our thoughts in their tracks and ask, "Do I want to download worldly thoughts, or do I want to meditate?" This simple reminder can get us back on track to repeating simran and focusing our attention within. Every time thoughts intervene, we can ask ourselves whether we want to spend our meditation thinking or spend it being receptive to download whatever God wants to send us. If we can train ourselves to do this, we will form a habit. That habit will be that the mind remains stilled during meditation time. Then, we will see rapid results in our meditation and will swim in the ocean of love and bliss.

We have all day long when not meditating to spend time thinking. When we set aside time for meditation, we do not want to waste that time downloading thoughts of the world. We want to be open to download what God is sending us. When we are absorbed in the light and sound, we rise from consciousness of this world into spiritual consciousness in which we awaken to inner spiritual realms. We then soar through the astral, causal, and supracausal realms, until we reach the spiritual region of Sach Khand, from where the Source, God, emanates.

Receptivity—being like an empty cup, or being like a computer that downloads God—opens us up to receive the eternal treasures of God, and helps us swim in the ocean of unspeakable light, music, love, peace, joy, and bliss.

PERSONAL REFLECTION

Track your thoughts throughout the day. Note how much time is spent downloading the world and how much time is spent downloading God or spirituality. Make a commitment to increase daily time in which one is absorbed in God or the soul, and note any changes in your daily life.

9

RULING PASSION

To fan our flame to merge into the Eternal Flame takes a ruling passion. A ruling passion gives us the desire to stick with something until we reach our goal. After we learn meditation on the light and sound through the grace of the Master, lead an ethical life, and stay receptive to downloading God, the next challenge is to stick to our spiritual practices daily for accelerated results. The ability to stay focused and committed to daily practice requires developing a ruling passion. When something is routine and mechanical it is easy for us to either stop devoting continual time to it or to give it up entirely. A ruling passion is a helping factor for success in meditation. The ocean of love, light, and bliss is waiting; we need to have a ruling passion to dive in and swim.

There are many examples of how a ruling passion is needed for success in various professions.

An electrical engineer puts in many years of study to invent and design technical or medical equipment, computers, cars, airplanes, or spacecraft. To master this field of work great passion is needed to stick with it.

In this connection, there is an example from the life of Thomas Edison. He was determined to find a filament for the incandescent light bulb. He had unsuccessfully tried 999 materials as filaments.

When someone said to him, "You have failed 999 times," Edison replied, "I have not failed. I have discovered 999 materials that won't work."

There is another example of Thomas Edison's dedication. He used to work for long hours in a laboratory. His wife was concerned he was working too hard without a vacation.

When he returned home from work one day, his wife said, "Dear, I am concerned that you are working yourself to death. You have worked long and hard without a rest. You must go on vacation."

Thomas Edison asked, "Where on earth would I go?"

His wife said, "Decide where you would rather be than any other place on Earth."

Thomas Edison thought for a moment and said, "Okay, I will go tomorrow."

The next morning, his wife saw him packing his travel bag. When the coach arrived to pick him up, she eagerly listened to find out where he was going to go on his vacation. To her surprise, she heard him say to the driver, "I am going on vacation to the place I would rather be than anywhere on Earth."

"Where is that?" asked the driver.

Thomas Edison told him, "Take me to my laboratory."

This anecdote shows the kind of passion needed to achieve greatness in one's field.

Think about how much education is required

to become a doctor. Students go through many years of medical school, internship, and residency. To have people entrust their lives to someone for diagnosis, operations, or treatment requires that they undergo many years of study. To stick with years of grueling study to remember every part of the human anatomy, every medicine and drug, every illness, and learn how to properly diagnose and treat patients requires a ruling passion to stick with it until the field is mastered.

Those in the field of education need many years of study to learn how to teach. They need to know the subject matter well enough to convey it to others. They are trained how to teach students of all ages to keep them motivated and inspired to learn. To stay with such a difficult field requires passion.

A ruling passion is needed in the arts. Artists work hard to learn how to express themselves through paintings. It takes many years of practice to produce a work of art.

Writers spend many years perfecting their craft. They have to learn the rules of grammar and the art of writing. It takes years of practice to develop the skill and talent to write a book or articles that inspire and motivate people. One needs a command of the language—an understanding of the various meanings of words, symbolism, metaphors, and analogies—to say things differently. Think of how hard it is to express the same idea in a new way. It takes a ruling passion to become a writer.

Poets spend many years perfecting their art. They need to know the various types of poetry and the rules for each. Poets have to convey an idea or meaning using only a few words and in new ways to express ideas about which others have written before them. They need to be able to take examples from life, from nature, from the entire human experience and put them together to express their ideas or feelings in a given poetic format.

Musicians need to perfect their knowledge of music and apply it to an instrument, singing, or writing music. Think of how many hours of practice it takes to learn to play the instrument without any mistakes. It takes years and a ruling passion to be a musician.

Parents have a passion to take care of their children for at least eighteen years. To feed, clothe, and play with them; teach them to be good people; and care for them when they are sick takes a tremendous ruling passion.

In professional sports, athletes need a ruling passion to be the best to compete at that level. Millions of children play sports for fun, but how many make it to the professional level or become a sports legend? If we look at any of the great athletes, we find that they practice the same drill for many hours a day until it becomes second nature. One needs passion to excel in this field.

If passion is needed in the mundane areas of life, think of how much passion is needed to find God. To understand how to develop a ruling passion for spiritual progress, we can think of the Olympics.

In the Olympics, athletes compete from all over the world for a gold medal in sports, such as swimming, gymnastics, running, skiing, and many others. They want the gold medal to show they are the best in the world.

If we analyze what sets apart a gold medalist from those who get the silver or bronze medals, those who finish as runners-up, or those who never even make the Olympics, we find certain qualities make someone go from good to great. We can incorporate these traits into our own lives as we pursue excellence in any field, including spirituality.

OLYMPIC GOLD MEDALISTS FOCUS ON THEIR GOAL

The first quality Olympic heroes have is the ability to focus one hundred percent of their attention on the goal. When Olympic champions are interviewed they often describe how their entire life was based on the ruling passion of winning their goal. Some began preparing for the Olympics at ages three, four, or five or older, and they spent every waking moment of their lives focused on winning the gold medal. They did not drift from one thing to another; they set a goal and stuck to it without wavering. They put all their attention into that one activity. Their focus was not just on participation, but also on winning and being the best.

Athletes are trained to want to make only top scores and break all records. Some swimmers who have broken the world record for winning the most gold medals have described how they focused their entire lives on increasing their swimming speed. Think of how many times they have to go back and forth in a pool, timing themselves, and then speeding it up again and again to break previous records. It takes total focus to train the body and mind to perform accurately and quickly.

The same happens with champion divers. They have to perfect the art of jumping off a diving board, and doing a back flip, while spinning two or three times, straightening out their body, and landing in the water at a perfectly vertical angle with little water splash. They have to be totally focused on this goal to repeat the sequence until they reach perfection.

Look at volleyball players. Once, the United States women's team was unbeatable in over one hundred games. Their eyes, mind, and body were so focused on the incoming volleyball, that they would actually dive to the ground to get under the ball and punch it up with their fists to get it high enough for the other team player to hit it over the net. Think of the focus to be able to dive fast enough to get under a ball that has almost landed, before it touches the sand. What incredible focus one needs to be able to do this no matter how hard or how fast or where the ball lands.

As one analyzes the performance of those who win a gold medal from those who do not, one sees a high level of focus that helps them achieve the gold.

PASSION AND DRIVE OF OLYMPIC WINNERS TO ACHIEVE THE GOAL AND THE GOLD

Not only do gold medalists have one hundred percent focus on the goal, but also they are filled with a ruling passion and drive to achieve it. None of the gold medalists are lackadaisical in their attitudes. They are not working in a bored, humdrum way for their gold. They wake up each day excited about what they are doing. They are pumped and full of energy and life, with a passion to perfect their skills.

We can see this ruling passion in sports players who love what they are doing. They are excited about getting up to practice. They are so excited about it that for them it is not work; it is fun and enjoyment.

The gold medal swimmers love to swim. The gold medal divers love to dive. The gold medal runners love to run. Without that passion, how would they put in the time necessary to excel at their sport? Passion and drive are key ingredients in making a gold medalist.

TIME COMMITMENT OF OLYMPIC WINNERS TO EXCEED THE TIME SPENT BY OTHERS

The difference between an average athlete and a great one is also related to time spent in perfecting the skill. Some people may have a goal and love their sport, but fail to put in enough time to stand out at it. Gold medalists put much more time into their sport than those who do not even make it to the Olympics.

Look at the mechanics of this. For the body to perform at such high speeds or to be able to do twists, turns, and rotations while suspended in the air requires an incredible degree of synchronization of the body and mind. The brain has to use the senses to judge where the body is in space and to be able to direct the muscles of the body to split-second timing to perform accurately. For this to happen, those connections between the brain cells and the cells that run the rest of the body have to work on automatic pilot. To do this takes training and repetition. It is not just doing it once or twice that makes someone perfect. One has to repeat this hundreds and thousands of times until the body and brain can perform the feats automatically.

Olympic winners put in the maximum possible time to perfect their sports. They are the first ones at the gym to practice, and they are the last ones to leave. They may be seen practicing on weekends, on holidays, even in the middle of the night. They are consumed by the sport. The amount of time the athletes put in is rewarded by their bodies being able to do what they want them to do on command.

OLYMPIC WINNERS HAVE THE DISCIPLINE TO DO WHAT IT TAKES TO BE THE BEST

One can have a goal and a ruling passion for the goal. One can also put in the time to be a winner. There is another ingredient to winning that is important and that is having the discipline to do what it takes to be the best. One can show up for practice twelve hours a day, but the discipline of doing what is required during those hours is what makes a winner.

For example, think of Olympic sports heroes. There are certain exercise routines that take hours to perform and need to be followed exactly for maximum results. They might have to do many repetitive drills such as push-ups, running in place, or stretching that are not as exciting as playing the game, but are needed to hone the muscles and movements. There is discipline involved in keeping to the time schedule and tasks needed for practice.

Some sports require discipline when it comes to diet. For example, jockeys are required to be light, so they have to eat fewer calories. In sports that require muscle bulk, athletes need to eat certain foods, whether they like them or not. The stamina to run may require certain nutrients, which means athletes must watch their diets. It is not easy staying on any diet, whether to lose weight, gain weight, or watch one's blood sugar. When that athlete goes out with friends to a party, he or she may have to avoid certain foods, which takes discipline.

Sports ban the use of steroids, illegal drugs, and underage drinking. Thus, some athletes who get caught are eliminated from the competition. It takes discipline for them to observe the restrictions on drugs and alcohol when friends are offering it.

Coaches of Olympic gold medalist may require them to observe a set schedule of exercise and rest. They may have to get a certain number of hours of sleep or rest each night, which also involves discipline, especially when others are out partying all night.

Track the careers of the Olympic winners and one finds them following a disciplined life to reach their dreams.

OLYMPIC WINNERS FOCUS ON
THEIR OWN ACHIEVEMENT AND NOT
WHAT OTHERS ARE DOING

Many times when interviewed about how they prepared for their win, champions offer the same reply: "I had to focus on my game. I had to focus on what I do best." They were not concerned with what others were doing. They knew that if they did what they were supposed to do they had a chance at winning.

Those who do not win become caught up in thinking about what others are doing. One could sometimes see someone ahead in a race. Yet when that person turns his or her head to see another racer catch up, this distraction causes the one who is ahead to fall behind. We see horses that watch other horses sometimes trip and fall. For this reason, blinders are put on a horse to keep the animal on track so it is not distracted by others.

Athletes on a gymnastics team who watch other teammates perform before their own turn comes may see their friend make an error. This may make the gymnast upset and feel the pain of disappointment of their teammate so strongly that his or her own ability is affected. When the athlete focuses on someone else, his or her own performance suffers.

Winners stay fixed on what they are doing and not on what others are doing. In this way, they give their best and do not lose precious seconds looking at everyone else.

OLYMPIC GOLD MEDALISTS DO NOT
LET OBSTACLES STAND IN THEIR WAY

Often, gold medalists faced uphill battles against many obstacles in their lives to achieve the gold. They may have suffered physical pain, emotional pain from criticism of others, or financial setbacks.

Many gold medalists suffered falls resulting in broken bones or torn muscles. Did that stop them? No, they were back in action as soon as possible. Some people won gold medals while performing with colds, flu, and fevers. Some competed with their legs or arms wrapped up because they had not completely healed. They rose above and competed despite their physical pain.

Many athletes have faced criticism and ridicule from others who may have said, "You must be crazy! What makes you think you can win a gold medal in the Olympics!" Family and friends may have tried to dissuade the athlete from competing by putting him or her down or saying the athlete does not have the right stuff. Gold medalists work through the criticism of others and stay focused despite outer challenges.

Many other obstacles can deter an athlete. Some face great financial challenges. It costs money to have a coach, to practice, to get the right equipment, and to pay for membership in certain sports training facilities. Over many years, these costs become daunting. The parents of one gold medalist had to mortgage their house several times to pay the fees of practicing. Where there is a will, there is a way for winners.

OLYMPIC WINNERS DO NOT LET
FAILURES SIDETRACK THEM

Many athletes have a defeatist attitude. If they cannot do it well the first time around, they give up. The first time athletes lose a race they take it as a sign that they do not have a chance. What sets Olympic gold medalists apart is that they do not let failure stop them, but learn from their failures. Winners will look at videotape of their performance to spot their errors and fix them. If they fall, they get back up on their feet and try again. If they do not win the first time, they try again. They take failure as a challenge to overcome and use it as an incentive to try even harder and keep going.

Olympians who are runners-up, or only made silver or bronze, may return four years later to try again for the gold. Sometimes they get it on their second or third try. They do not let failure sidetrack them from their goal.

OLYMPIC GOLD MEDALISTS
HAVE FULL CONCENTRATION

Watch any gold medalist perform and one finds an almost superhuman ability to concentrate and focus. Before the competition, the athlete is mentally focused, visually rehearsing the required movements repeatedly to set the mind in gear. Focusing within, the athlete does not get distracted by anyone. During the performance, he or she maintains one hundred percent focus on the task.

When one watches those who make mistakes in gymnastics, diving, or any athletic routine, one can sometimes notice a moment of distraction set in. The athlete has lost focus. Those who win are able to maintain full concentration for the entire duration of their performance. This is one of the keys to going from good to great.

DEVELOPING QUALITIES OF AN OLYMPIC CHAMPION TO REACH SPIRITUAL GOALS

All the above qualities needed to make an Olympic winner in the field of sports also apply to reaching our spiritual goals. By looking at the examples of saints and Masters who reach the heights of spirituality, we can see what it takes for us also to reach the spiritual goal of union with the Divine.

Saints exemplify the qualities that make a gold medalist. Their achievement is the Olympics of meditation and spirituality. They attain the goal that every person who meditates is trying to attain—reuniting the soul with God. Their lives exemplify all the qualities an Olympic gold medalist needs to win the gold. If we examine their lives from this angle, it gives us a blueprint of what we need to do to also achieve the same goal in spirituality and meditation.

In the physical Olympics there can only be one gold medalist, but in the field of meditation and spirituality each of us can win the gold medal. For example, in practicing meditating on the inner light and sound, winning the gold medal means being able to soar on the current of light and sound through all the higher realms and reach the abode of God, Sach Khand, where our soul merges with God. It is not restricted to an Olympics every four years—we can participate in this Olympic 24/7 and can attain the gold at any time. The question is: Why wait? Why not complete the course now?

Saints have one hundred percent focus on their chosen goal. They never swerve from that goal. They stick with it until they attain union of the soul with God.

From the moment they search for the answers to the mystery of life and death, Masters have a ceaseless ruling passion and drive to achieve that goal. They are fully committed to follow the spiritual teachings to the letter. They are full of passion and zeal, another gold medal trait that helps them achieve union with God in their lifetime.

Saints make a time commitment to meditation and spirituality far beyond that made by many others, which is a key component in their success in finding God. They teach positive mysticism in which they earn an honest living, and many marry and have children. Along with this, they find time to meditate and perform selfless service. They make a time commitment to meditation and service and stick to it no matter what.

Saints exemplify discipline. They do whatever is necessary to be successful in achieving the goal of finding God. This success depends on meditation, which they do daily for the longest possible time. Along with this, they also live up to the ethical virtues. This involves leading a life of nonviolence, truthfulness, purity, humility, and selfless service. They are the epitome of nonviolence. Their ethical life involves them living on a strict vegetarian diet, avoiding all meat, fish, fowl, and eggs, both fertile and infertile, and not partaking of alcohol and hallucinogenic or intoxicating drugs.

Saints stay focused on their spiritual goals no matter what others are doing. They are not concerned with what others do; they keep their attention on what they have to do. They never get involved in criticism or backbiting even though others may have done so. This focus on their own spiritual progress keeps them from falling into the trap of wasting time on what others are doing. This quality helps them use their precious breaths of life to attain union with God.

Saints do not let any obstacles stand in the way of their achieving spiritual goals. Neither physical pain, nor negativity of others, nor any other setback stops them from their chosen path. Think of the stamina needed to meditate for long hours, yet they do so no matter what. Think of the grueling schedule of career, family, meditation, and seva they observe, yet they never become sidetracked. Think of the labor of love they put in to do selfless service: after a long day's work, they engage in physical, intellectual, or spiritual seva to help others. They stay up late doing selfless service, often working the whole night. As tired as their body may be after working at their physical job all day, they serve others and attend to meditation.

Saints have full concentration and focus in meditation.

They say that if we sit accurately in meditation, we will soar within. They stay with their meditation for many hours daily and make great spiritual progress. When it is time to meditate, they do not skip it to gossip or waste time. They stick with their schedule no matter what.

Saints never let failures sidetrack them. They experience the same ups and downs of life that everyone goes through, but never let that stop them from meditating no matter what. Despite hardships, they do not give up; they keep going, stay true to the ethical virtues, meditate, and do seva, despite hardships, until they achieve the spiritual goal.

HOW WE CAN WIN THE OLYMPICS OF SPIRITUALITY

Meditation on the inner light and sound requires full concentration and focus. Ultimately, we reach the purely spiritual realm of Sach Khand in which we become one with God. This is a journey of love and ecstasy. When the soul reunites with God, we are immersed eternally in love and bliss. This is the gold medal of spirituality. Oneness with God is the goal.

If we apply the dedication of Olympic gold medalists and follow the example of the spiritual Masters, we will have a blueprint so that we too can win the gold medal of spirituality. What one person can do so can another.

To illustrate the kind of ruling passion needed to find God there is an anecdote about a young man who wanted to learn how to meditate. He visited a holy man who was meditating on a riverbank in India. The young man watched quietly as the saint sat in silent meditation.

When the saint had completed meditating and opened his eyes, the young man approached him and asked, "Can you teach me how to meditate?" The holy man studied the young man for a few moments. Suddenly, the holy man grabbed the man's head and shoved him face down into the water of the river. He held the young man's face underwater for some moments until the man began struggling and flailing to free himself so he could breathe. When the young man's struggle became desperate to surface for air, the saint finally let go of him.

The young man, gasping for breath, was shocked, and asked, "Why would you try to drown me?"

The holy man said, "You asked me to teach you how to meditate. This was your first lesson."

The young man said, "I don't understand what drowning someone has to do with teaching them how to meditate."

The holy man then explained, "True meditation means doing so with that same longing you had when you were gasping for air. When our thirst and ruling passion for God is as great as our thirst for air, that is the stage in which we will merge back in God."

On the spiritual path, thirst for God brings us to a saint to find answers to the mysteries of life. Thirst for God drives us to abide by the requirements for initiation into the light and sound of God. Thirst for God drives us to follow the instructions to meditate. Thirst for God impels us to perform selfless service and lead an ethical life. Thirst for God drives us to put in time for daily meditation until we reach our spiritual goal.

If we are already blessed with such a thirst, we can be grateful. If we do not have it, let us develop it. We can do so by being in the physical company of the Master or imbibing the spiritual radiation he is sending to us in a satsang we may attend anywhere in the world. We can develop that thirst by doing selfless service, which cleanses us of our ego and self. We can develop that thirst through daily introspection to help us develop ethical qualities. Finally, we can develop that thirst by sitting in meditation. Each spark of divine light we receive and each celestial sound we hear serve to develop in us that insatiable thirst for more and more until we too will be rewarded by a divine thirst and ruling passion to attain the Olympic gold of reaching God.

PERSONAL REFLECTION

List times in your life when you had a ruling passion for a goal. What was the goal and how did you stay committed to its attainment? Reflect on your goal to experience God. What can you do to develop a ruling passion to achieve the spiritual goal of life?

10

LIVING IN LOVE

Along with receptivity and a ruling passion, we need a burning love to merge our individual fire into the all-consuming eternal flame of the Divine. Love is a fuel that further ignites the fire until it expands into the radiant light of God.

FINDING TRUE LOVE

A basic need of every human being is to love and be loved. When psychologists speak of the basic human needs of food, clothing, shelter, and safety they also add the need for love.

People normally look in the outer world for love from their parents, siblings, and relatives. As they grow older, they seek love from their friends; in young adulthood, they seek the love of companions, their spouse, and their children. Unfortunately, sometimes in life, we learn that those loves can be fleeting. Relationships change; children move away; parents die. At some point the loves of this world bring sorrow at their loss.

This loss of love often turns us to God for relief from the suffering. When God hears our cry, God brings us to someone who can show us that we always have a permanent love within us. A Master connects us to the love of God, which is eternal.

Masters who have come through the ages have shown a way to find lasting love. They teach us meditation so we can find God's love within us. Because we cannot see God with our outer eyes, a Master teaches us how to find God with our inner eye.

When we come to a spiritual path, we experience the love of God. God is not experienced through the intellect. God is love, and the soul within us is also love. To experience God, we have to strip off the layers that keep us from experiencing divine love.

When people come to a Master, they can drink of that love. The Master radiates God's love to us. It comes automatically from the spiritual radiation of the Master and penetrates into our soul.

When we go to any worldly lecture by a speaker, we come away with intellectual knowledge. We learn about a certain topic. When we go to a spiritual Master, we receive more than intellectual information. While we get the theory of the teachings by word of mouth, we also receive an uplifting experience of the soul. The eyes of the Master are pouring out the blissful love of God. By being in the Master's presence, the elevating experience comes naturally. That uplifting boost is the energy that pulls our attention up from the body to the eye-focus. A Master's spiritually charged attention stirs us from within so the sensory currents begin withdrawing from awareness of the physical world and our body to awareness of the spiritual realms and our soul. This beautiful, rapturous experience of divine charging uplifts the soul. We become soaked in the most exquisite love that permeates our whole being. When we get even a taste of that bliss, we want to soar with it until it bathes us completely.

Spiritual bliss pulls our mind from the distractions of the world that keep us from self-knowledge and God-realization. The magnetizing power of God's love is so strong it fills us with divine intoxication.

People become involved in various pastimes and entertainments of this world. Among these are also harmful addictions like drugs, alcohol, gambling, and other cravings that can be so powerful that people cannot break the habits with willpower.

Just think of how powerful is the ecstasy of divine love that it makes worldly pastimes seem pale and insipid. God's love is more fulfilling that any of the pursuits of this world.

GLANCE OF DIVINE LOVE

The glance of divine love, or *darshan* of a Master, is so powerful that without it, those who have tasted it long to receive it again. When separated from that glance, the disciple suffers longing. Anyone who has suffered separation from a loved one knows how each minute, and each second, feels like an eternity. Being without that glance is like depriving a child from its mother's milk. The child cries until nourished. When this longing becomes intense, it pulls our attention from wanting worldly gains that are temporary to a quest for divine love within.

When one receives such a glance, the attention gets a boost to soar within. For this reason, people travel the lengths and breadth of the earth to see a Master, or wait to have his darshan. Their souls want to drink from the glance of love. They have realized the impermanence of everything in the world and know that lasting love emanates from the divine glance flowing through the Master. They are no longer enslaved by their minds to want things of this world. They become conscious of their true selves, their souls, which yearn for oneness with God. They are opened up to the real nature of their souls, which are made of the same essence as God. Thus, they want to be reunited with God. They experience the radiation of God's love through a glance of grace.

The glance of grace is like sweet nectar flowing into the cup of one's soul. It is an all-pervading sweetness that permeates one's being, filling one with a life force that uplifts the soul.

Some people try to get intoxicated by drinking alcohol or taking intoxicating drugs. Why do they do that? They are looking for an upliftment. What they do not realize is that the most intoxicated one can get from alcohol or drugs is not even a fraction of the intoxication experienced when tasting God's love within. Plus, the chemical intoxication does not last and has serious side effects. The intoxication from God has only beneficial effects. People who once taste of Godly love want to be in that state again. It uplifts one far beyond this physical world to carry the soul through regions of bliss.

The glance of grace is not a physical experience. It is a jumping-off point to help boost us in meditation, making it easier because the time spent in stilling our mind is shortened. The Master's penetrating gaze can open up our heart and soul to receive God's wondrous beauty. If we receive his glance, it opens up the doorway into the enchantments waiting for us in the beyond. Lucky are those souls who get the glance in its fullness.

When we leave the assembly of the Master in which he has poured out pitchers of divine ecstasy, we are wiped clean of negative thoughts and emptied of desires, and we bubble over with Godly love. The slate of our mental wranglings has been wiped clean and on our heart the beautiful calligraphy of God's poetry is engraved.

Transformed by the power of his radiation, we are filled with love and want to love everyone. We become like a pipe through which Godly love flows out to the world.

The lessons we learn from a Master are those taught without words. There are moments in which four eyes, the two eyes of the Master and the two eyes of the disciple, merge and they become one. The soul is no longer a distinct entity embodied in the physical form of the disciple. The soul dives into the Master's eyes and swims in them. Since the Master is merged with the Divine, the disciple experiences divinity. When oneness takes place, only bliss remains. That is the power of divine love; it makes us want more until we merge with that ecstasy—an ecstasy that fills us with bliss.

That is why receptive people enjoy sitting in the presence of a saint. They melt into the bliss of the Master's eyes and do not want to leave.

GLANCE OF LOVE FROM WITHIN

We can also receive the glance of divine love from within. In meditation, the radiant or ethereal form of the spiritual Master appears to us in all effulgence and radiates the love of God. The radiation pouring from his glance of love uplifts our soul on the light and sound, propelling us through the higher regions until we eventually enter the purely spiritual realm of Sach Khand.

To achieve union of our soul with God, we must have yearning for God. We need to spend many hours in meditation. When our desire is intense and sincere, God fulfills our prayers. By going within through meditation, our soul will find delight in the Lord. Our long journey will be complete.

When we meditate, we experience intoxication. There is bliss waiting within that can uplift our soul. For some who are trying to perfect the meditation practice, it may take many hours to still the mind to withdraw one's attention. The grace of the Master is such that when we see his radiant form, it has the power to uplift the soul instantaneously. One loving glance from the Master can immediately put the mind to rest and give it the calm and stillness for the soul to withdraw. The soul experiences a beverage-like intoxication flowing from within and the attention rises up to the eye-focus. When one sits in meditation in such a state, one can achieve results.

EVERLASTING LOVE

People do not want a love that is fleeing. They do not want a fleeting glance or a brief meeting. They want an everlasting glance, an everlasting meeting—to be in an eternal state of union with their Beloved. They have realized there is no lasting love in this world. Even the best and closest of relationships in this physical world must ultimately end, because that is the nature of this world. Our physical forms are made to fade. Some people live to one month of age, some to one year, some to five years, some to ten years, twenty, fifty, and some to a hundred years or more. However, our physical end is inevitable. When we realize life's impermanence, we seek a love that will not end. We can find it by swimming in the ocean of eternal love.

There is a story about a king who held a bazaar. The king told all his subjects to pick whatever they liked. Almost all the subjects of the kingdom scurried about picking trinkets. They picked gold, diamonds, expensive clothing, or luxury items. Only one girl did not select anything. The king noticed that the bazaar was going to close and approached her asking her to choose something. She then proceeded to put her hand on the king, choosing him for her own. Why? She knew that the other trinkets were not lasting. Once the fair was over, there would be no more access to the gifts of the bazaar. The king had the power to hold many such fairs; by choosing the king, she had access to everything in the fair now and in the future.

Similarly, when we choose to love God, we love the one who grants us all the gifts and will never leave us. It is not a temporary love—God is eternal. When we love God, we love a Beloved who is with us even beyond the gates of death. We will go to God's abode and live in eternal wedlock with our true Beloved.

LIVING IN A LAND OF LOVE

Sant Darshan Singh Ji Maharaj wrote the following verse:

> *I am seeking a land of love*
> *Where there is only talk of peace and kindness.*

This verse describes how a disciple is seeking a land of love. The disciple has lived countless lives of suffering and has seen the pain that one can undergo in the world. He or she is sick of gossip and hearing the complaints of others, exhausted from arguments, and fed up with violence and hatred. The disciple is tired of being in a land of ego fights, power struggles and territorial battles and wants to live in a land of love.

The disciple seeks a place in which the talk is of peace and kindness. The disciple wants to speak and hear sweet and loving words and to enjoy the company of others in a harmonious state. The disciple wonders, "Is there such a place and where can it be found?"

Such a place the disciple is not finding in worldly company. There seems to be nothing but talk of problems. The disciple wants the company of someone filled with peace. He or she can find that in the company of a spiritual Master who has realized God. Such a saint is filled with love, being merged with the source of all love, with God. Thus, in such company only talk of the love of God is taking place. In such company, only kindness is exhibited.

When one comes to a gathering with the Master, one only wants to experience a land of love. There are many opportunities for moments in which one can be transported to this land.

People come to enjoy the peace of being in the Master's presence. They do not come for gossip. When they are sitting in the Master's presence in a gathering such as satsang, or are waiting for darshan, they do not want to talk about things not loving. In fact, some do not want to talk at all. They remain absorbed within to catch as much of the Master's glances and radiation as they can. They do not want to be distracted by talk of worldly things.

In this regard there was once a princess named Laila who was always absorbed in the love and remembrance of her earthly beloved, Majnu. Once she was going to a holy place to pray. She was so lost in her thoughts of Majnu that she did not notice when she stepped on the prayer mat of a holy man. As soon as she had stepped on the mat, the holy man jumped up and began scolding her for her sacrilegious act. She was startled out of her reverie by this commotion.

He said, "How could you have committed such a

disrespectful act of walking on the prayer mat while I was praying?"

Apologetically, she said, "I am sorry, but I was so lost in the thoughts of my earthly beloved that I did not notice where I was going." But then, with wisdom, she remarked, "I just wonder, O holy one, that if I could be so lost in my worldly beloved that I did not notice where I was walking, how could you be so lost in remembrance of God, and yet you could still notice me walking on your mat? If you were truly lost, you would not have noticed me at all."

Thus, if we become more like Laila rather than the holy man in the story who was more interested in criticizing the actions of others than being absorbed in God, then we too, like Laila, will have union with our Beloved.

If we want to be in the land of love, we should derive maximum benefit from our time with the Master. We need to come as empty cups ready to receive a sip of love. Think of the time with the Master as moments in which we enter the temple within. If we clear our mind of thoughts of the past or future or of the world and be in a state of loving receptivity, we would be open to receive the grace pouring out. Instead of being critical, complaining, and filled with anger, greed, violence, and ego, we can act with nonviolence, kindness, and selflessness. If we become the empty cup waiting to be filled, in a receptive state, we could swim in divine bliss.

The disciple knows there is nothing in the world that will satisfy him or her. There is nothing else in the world that brings lasting intoxication. The disciple has scoured the earth looking for happiness but finds it not and knows that the only lasting joy is in divine love.

The disciple then seeks out the company of the Master. That is where one sees the glimpses of hope and finds relief from the sufferings of the world.

The disciple also knows the importance of going within through meditation. The inner journey begins with the inner light. Absorption in the light leads the soul deeper and further within. Ultimately, we cross inner vistas and reach the radiant form of the Master. The Master's ethereal form has the same physical features as the outer form, but is more radiant. It is more intoxicating than the physical form and brings relief from the sorrows of the world. The radiant form serves as our guide to take us on the inner journey to the eternal Home in the land of love.

SWIM IN THE OCEAN OF LOVE

When we swim in the crystal clear, pure ocean of God, we can see the reflection of our true self or soul. There is no grime or dirt to muddy it. We can see to the depth of the ocean, undistracted by anything that keeps our attention from the calm of the water. Its loving waves lap against us. There are no attractions to lead us away from our peace. Instead of transitory pleasures of the outer world, we enjoy the eternal bliss of God. There is no ill effect from having too much love. When we swim in the ocean of God, we experience ecstasy.

A blissful pool of divine water is within all the time. We can dip into it anytime. When we tap into this pool, we are free from worries. We enter total relaxation. Its soothing waters caress our being, washing away the tensions of the mind and body. When our soul is bathed, bliss also permeates our mind and body. Mind is under control so it does not disturb our tranquility at the level of the soul.

The origin of the word "spa" means "taking of the waters." On a holiday people often like to go to a spa and swim in a pool or soak in a hot tub to relax. We have our own internal spa fed by the waters of God that soothe our soul. When our soul is soothed, our body and mind are naturally at rest.

If this divine pool is always within us, why don't we take a swim in it? Unfortunately, we are swimming with the mind. Swimming with the mind is like swimming with the sharks. Its intent is to devour us. If we opt to swim with the mind, the lovely pool becomes muddied. The calm waters turn into a mud hole. It is thick, sticky, and heavy, and it entraps us.

When I was a child I accidentally stepped into quicksand. It was a horrifying experience to feel my body being pulled down deeper into the muddy ground. Someone saw me, grabbed me, and pulled me out. When we swim in the pool of the mind, this is what happens. The mud pulls us down and on our own we cannot get out.

What has caused the pool to be muddy? The mind is filled with desires that lead us into ego, lust, anger, attachment, and greed. When our pool is filled with the mind, we become stuck. We are burdened with more problems, and our lives are filled with stress.

Rather than swimming with the mind, we should swim with God. When we swim with God, we are satisfied. We fall in love with God and lose our ego. We are like those who are so in love that they forget themselves. We become so lost in God that we lose ourselves and become one with God.

It is said that a salt doll went into the ocean to take a dip. As soon as it stepped into the ocean, it dissolved into the ocean and became one with it. When we are immersed in God, we are like that salt doll. We dive into the ocean of God, and become immersed in it, losing ourselves in intoxication. It is not an annihilation of self, but an expansion of our self to be one with God and eternally permeated with bliss and love that knows no end.

When we swim with God, we do not have any desires for the sensual pleasures of the world, because the love of God is fulfilling. The bliss that permeates the soul when we swim with God is thousands of times greater than any worldly satisfaction.

When we swim with God we are filled with calm. We have no time or interest in judging others, because we are focused on being with our divine Beloved. A verse by Sant Darshan Singh Ji Maharaj says:

Those who are lost in divine intoxication,
Have no time to laugh at the condition
of others.

When we swim with God, we have everything and are content. There is nothing of this world that compares with the ecstasy of swimming with God. Our entire being, from the core of the soul, is ravished by God's divine love and embrace. Who would want to tear oneself away from an ocean of incredible love? No desires of the world can pull us away from that bliss. We realize that everything and everyone of this world is transitory. We know that one day we will pass away, or those we love will pass away. Only the soul and God are permanent. When we lose our attachment for the transitory world and attach ourselves to God, we gain permanent happiness. We realize that when we fall in love with God, we are with a Beloved who will be with us for eternity.

We can swim with God anytime we want. God has sent the Master to teach us how to swim in bliss. We can do so by meditating. Meditation is not just a mechanical process; it is diving into a pool of bliss. We focus our attention into the pool of love between our two eyebrows, and dive in. With our mind still, we plunge into the soothing waters of the divine Beloved and are in pure ecstasy.

Once Ramakrishna said to a disciple, "God is an ocean of bliss. Do you want to dive into it?"

The disciple said, "How?"

Ramakrishna said, "If there is a cup of syrup and you are a fly, where would you sit to drink the syrup?"

The disciple said, "I would sit on the edge of the syrup."

Ramakrishna then told him, "Why would you sit on the edge?"

The disciple said, "If I go in deeper, I will drown

and lose my life."

Ramakrishna said, "But in the ocean of God there is no fear of death. It is an ocean of immortality. By plunging into it, one becomes immortal. Dive in. One does not lose his consciousness by diving into the ocean of God. Do not sit on the edge, but dive in!"

Through meditation we plunge into the heart of the ocean and are immersed in the ocean of love.

Even when we are not meditating, we can be swimming in ecstasy. How? We can keep our attention on the divine Beloved all hours of the day and night. While driving, while working with our hands or body, while cooking food, while eating, while exercising, or doing any other activities, we can remember God. When we go to satsang, if we are receptive, we can let the waters of divine love flow into us. Swimming with God fills us with love, and we become the abode of nonviolence, truthfulness, purity, humility, and selfless service. By diving into the pool of God we can swim eternally in bliss.

PERSONAL REFLECTION

Reflect on moments in life when you experienced love. Reflect on how joyous your life would be if you could live in such a state all the time. Sit in meditation to get in touch with the divine love within.

11

GRATITUDE TO THE GIVER

The Eternal Flame shines within us when we are receptive, have a ruling passion, and live in love. It is further fanned by having gratitude to God, the Giver. Gratitude is another gift God gives to accelerate our spiritual progress.

PRAYERS TO GOD

There was a movie in which a man had an opportunity to take God's job. He found out quickly that God is bombarded with endless complaints and prayers from billions of people requesting things all at the same time. In fact, in this humorous movie, when God checked the email, there were millions of email messages of complaints and requests. There were few who thanked God for the good they received.

It may be a humorous film, but it has truth in it. We focus more on what God has not given than what God has given us. If we were to fill out a thank you note to God for all the good we received, we would discover that we have received much.

There is a story about God sending two angels to Earth to listen to the prayers of humanity. One angel was asked to collect the prayers asking God for something. The other angel was asked to collect the prayers of thanksgiving and gratitude.

The two angels were given large baskets to collect the prayers and descended to earth to begin their task. They agreed to meet back in a month with their results. The angel collecting prayers asking God for something became extremely busy. Many people prayed to God to help them earn more money or get a windfall. Others prayed for cures for their illnesses. Many prayed for improved health for their children, spouse, parents, siblings, relatives, or friends. The angel also collected prayers for the latest computer, exquisite jewelry, expensive clothing, and new toys. There were so many prayers asking for things.

The angel contacted the other angel and asked, "Is the basket of prayers filled?"

In the meantime, the other angel traveled far and wide looking to fill the basket with prayers of thankfulness. One day passed, two days passed, three days passed, but no prayers of gratitude were heard. The angel visited young people and elderly people, men and women, people of all countries, all religions, and all economic levels. Still not a prayer of thankfulness was heard. All that this angel heard were prayers asking for things. The angel contacted the other angel to find out whether that angel's basket of prayers was being filled.

"Oh, yes, I have not only filled one basket, but have filled a truck," said the angel.

For the rest of the month, the two angels fulfilled their mission and were ready to return to God. The angel collecting prayers of requests had a loaded truck. When their time came to a close, the angel collecting prayers of thankfulness had only a few.

When God was presented with their findings, God sighed.

"This is nothing new," said God. "You now have a taste of what it is like being God. People are always praying for something from Me, which is all right because at least they are thinking of Me. But few ever thank Me."

This story illustrates the human condition. People request others to do something for them, but how many people take an equal amount of time to thank them? Similarly, we pray to God for things we want. How many of us take the time to thank God?

The post office receives many letters from children addressed to Santa Claus before Christmas. Yet, after Christmas, children do not typically send a letter to Santa thanking him for what they received.

GIFTS FROM THE GIVER

Let us recount the many things for which we owe our gratitude to God, the Giver.

First, we are extremely fortunate that our soul was born into a human body. If we look around at all the various species of life, we see what a difficult existence they have. They have a life in which they have to find shelter from the elements and live in fear of predators. While many people treat their pets as well as their own family members, pets are still enslaved. Even though there are now pet beauty salons, pet therapists, and pet yoga classes offered, animals lack the faculty that we have in which we can be conscious of who we are. Their lives are restricted to feelings and survival instincts. They cannot contemplate who they are, why they are here, and where they are going. We are fortunate that we have been born into the only species who can know ourselves and know God. For this, we should thank God.

How many thank God for our health? When we are in the throes of a serious illness or have an accident and are in pain, we send loud prayers to God to help us, to take away our pain and heal us. Yet, how many of us send prayers to God in gratitude for our health? We may utter a "Thank God," when our illness or our pain ends, but then we often do not thank God for each day thereafter that we are healthy.

A friend of one of the great woman saints, Rabia Basri, came to her with his head bandaged. When he moaned to God in pain, she asked him what was wrong. He said he had a severe headache.

She asked, "How long have you had the headache?" He said he had it for a day.

She asked him, "For how many days in your life have you gone without a headache?" He said he had not had a headache for most of his life.

She replied wisely, "For one day that you have a headache you complain to God, yet for the thousands of days in your life that you have not had a headache, have you ever thanked God?"

We may feel that God only exists when everything

goes our way. We ignore the good things such as our physical gifts, intellectual gifts, and emotional gifts from God. We forget that everything we receive comes from God. Instead, we set up a condition that we only believe there is a God if we get whatever we want. We take for granted what God has given to us and focus on what God has not given to us.

We may have had a job for twenty-five years, but the one time we are laid off due to a company downsizing we say there is no God. We may have had a loving family relationship for fifty years, but when one member passes away, we forget how long we enjoyed his or her company and instead blame God or say there is no good in our life. We may have been healthy for forty years, but the one major illness we have we say, "Why is this happening to me? There must not be any God." We may win all our sports games, but the one loss causes us to say, "God doesn't care about me." Think about the plight of God. With all that has been given to us, we blame God when one thing goes wrong. How would we think God feels when that happens? Few are grateful to God for the good they receive so that when something goes wrong they tell God, "It's okay, God. I still love You, I am grateful to You, and I know You are there. What happened must have been something that was best for me, or was due to my karma that I created, or is a part of nature and life and is okay, under Your will." How many people take such a grateful attitude to God?

There are people who undergo a tremendous amount of pain yet remain grateful and thank God on days they are pain-free. Most take good health for granted. Even if we have some physical problems or some pain we have to live with, we should thank God for what we still can do, whether it is waking up in the morning, or going to work, or finding some moments of enjoyment in our lives. If we spend time complaining to God about our physical condition, even though we can still function, we should look at those who have serious handicaps that make them dependent on others, and then reevaluate our own situation. Some people have handicaps, yet are so grateful they are alive or that their suffering is not worse. They are grateful to God for whatever blessings they do have. Let us thank God for our health and be grateful our ailments are not worse than they are. For each day that we are able to do our work, enjoy our family and friends, and meditate, thank God.

We should be grateful to God for our education. Education helps us have options in our life and career. We have choices on what subjects we want to learn and in which fields we wish to specialize. There are many who do not have choices and must take any work they find. Thank God daily for our education and how it helps us.

Have we ever thanked God for our spouse, our parents, or our children? We often find reasons to complain about those in our family, but we seldom realize how helpful it is to have a family. Some may be living alone now, but when they were growing up, they lived with family. Think about how difficult life would be without parents, a caretaker, siblings, a spouse, children, or relatives. Friends can help us only so far, but family members are committed to being there for us through thick and thin. When we are sick, they help us. When we have no money, they are there. They are there to listen to our problems and to help us. We often find reason to complain to God about our family members, but how many thank God that we have them? Often, we only appreciate them when we lose them through death or separation. Let us take time to thank God for them and also show them how much we appreciate them. When was the last time we told our close ones that we love and appreciate them? Let us add our thanks for our relationships to the basket of the angel collecting prayers of gratitude.

Developing gratitude begins with recognizing all the gifts we receive.

PHYSICAL GIFTS FROM GOD

We can start with the physical gifts from God. Each day the sun rises to bring light to the world so we can see. The sun gives us warmth. It provides nourishment to plants, which in turn give us food.

God has given us nature that abounds with food to eat and water to drink. The cycles of nature replenish the food and water supply. Think of how many billions of years this planet has been existence and the billions of life forms that have fed and drank from earth. So far the food and water has not run out. Similarly, the air supply has been sustaining life for billions of years. Think of how many people breathe in the oxygen from the air, and it has so far not run out. The plants continually supply the atmosphere with oxygen, as they thrive on the carbon dioxide waste that humans and animals exhale. What a remarkable system God has provided. Those are some items for which we can daily thank God.

We can thank God that systems are set in place to deliver food to our table through a network of stores. Labor is divided so we do not have to grow our own food. Water is delivered to our home through pipes. Waste is taken away through a sewage system. Our life is made easier by appliances that have been invented. Many of these appliances run on electricity supplied through a power plant sending energy to our home. We have telephones, televisions, and computers that run on wireless transmission. Each day we can thank God for innovations that make our life easier, speed up transportation, and make communication instantaneous. Gone are the days of pony express when a letter had to be sent by a courier traveling on foot or by horse, or by slow boat overseas that could take days, weeks, and months to arrive. With email, text messages, fax, and telephone we get communication the instant it is sent.

We can be grateful to God for the wondrous breakthroughs in medicine. Many people maintain their health through medicine, such as allopathic, naturopathic, Ayurvedic, homeopathic, or other means. We can thank God for every moment we feel healthy. If we think about our life, most of the time we were either healthy or in a state of bearable discomfort, so we could still go about our work and play. Although there have been some moments in which we suffered unbearable pain, they were few compared to the pain-free or bearable moments. Most of the time, the doctor or medicines helped us out of excruciating pain. If we were to write down the number of days we were healthy, we would fill up hundreds of thank you boxes to God for the blessings of good health.

INTELLECTUAL GIFTS FROM GOD

Besides physical blessings, we also have intellectual gifts from God. Life on the planet is not easy for the animals. Their life is one of survival. They live on instinct to get their food and to bear and protect their offspring. They struggle to survive. Humans have a brain and intellect to find ways to survive. We have an intellect to devise civilized ways of life. We learn a trade or career whereby others benefit from our skills. We have an interdependent society in which we can earn money for our work and use it to buy what we need. Otherwise, if we were each independent we would have to do everything for ourselves and our family. Through interdependence, we can have access to all the merchandise, supplies, and services we need in exchange for our providing a service or goods to others. We can thank God if we have a skill we can share and from which we can earn our livelihood. We can be grateful if we live in a society in which people set in place financial help, insurance, welfare, social security, or charities for times when we do not have a job. Have we ever thanked God for helping us get food each day?

EMOTIONAL GIFTS

We also have emotional gifts from God. Our emotional side thrives on love and bonding with others. Each of us has had parents or a caretaker, brothers and sisters, grandparents, aunts and uncles, or neighbors to provide us love as a child. Some may have had more love as a child, while others less, but almost every person can find a reason to thank God for someone in life. We may have love from a spouse, a beloved, or a dear friend. We may find relationship in our family, at work, with our neighbors, on a sports team, or in our places of worship. Humans thrive on connection, and we tend to form friendships. If we think about how many caring bonds we have formed, we can add those into our thank you boxes to God. We can thank God for these relationships that bring us love.

SPIRITUAL GIFTS OF GOD

We also have received spiritual gifts. This includes the gift of our soul longing for God. Many may feel God has forsaken them. They do not feel God in their lives. Some even deny the existence of God. Why? When we are so focused on our outer life, we do not see what is coming to us from our inner life. We are only facing in one direction.

Spiritually, we are blessed. Our soul is a part of God. Each of us is blessed with a way to find God who sits within us. In this search, some people stop at the level of going to their places of worship and reading scriptures.

For them, this is a beginning connection with God. Outer religious practices provide some time in which people can think about God, sing God's praises, and worship. These gifts focus our attention on God. However, for our soul to directly experience God requires more than outer worship. There is a part of us that wants to know God and is not satisfied with only reading about God in scriptures or doing outer practices to worship God. When we have a spiritual awakening in which we realize the need to find God, we begin to yearn to receive a firsthand experience of the spark of the Divine. We start a search for God and cannot rest until we meet God. We are no longer satisfied with the attractions of this world; we want something lasting.

God is gracious and works through spiritual Masters. Masters point the way back to God's Abode. A spiritual Master roams the earth ready to show seekers the way back to God. Masters are like lighthouses beaming out rays to invite our lost ships back to a safe harbor. If our eyes are facing the darkness and mist of the seas, we do not see the lighthouse. The moment we are threatened by storms, we turn our eyes in every direction, seeking the guiding light of the lighthouse. That moment is our spiritual awakening when we realize we cannot brave the stormy seas of life alone and need help. We do not know how to access God. The Master is a catalyst who puts us in touch with God through a process of initiation into the inner light and sound and teaches meditation on that current. Through meditation, our soul can travel on that divine current back to its true Source.

There are many reasons to be grateful for God's spiritual gifts. If we have awakened to the need to find God, that is a gift from God and is the first step on our journey Homeward. If we have met a living spiritual Master who can connect us to the light and sound, we can be grateful to God. If we receive initiation from the Master, then that is a gift for which we can be eternally grateful.

It is a great blessing to find a living Master. There are many benefits to having a Master. First, the Master gives us initiation so we can see and hear the light and sound of God. The Master serves as our inner guide through the spiritual regions until our soul safely reaches the region of all consciousness. The Master is our friend and companion to help us with our problems. He also takes over our karmic accounts accumulated during our past lifetimes. These karmas are the forces that bring the soul back into a life form in the three lower realms of creation so we can receive rewards for our good deeds and consequences for our bad deeds. We cannot escape this cycle until we have a zero balance. With the number of thoughts, words, and deeds we commit every second, it would be almost impossible to ever have a balance of zero. Thus, we keep returning to this realm.

Our past karmas are taken over by the Master at the time of initiation. Thus, we have only the karmas of this current life left to pay. Those who have been initiated have their karmic load placed in the hands of the Master. Our job is to ensure that we do not add to our karma in our remaining years so that when this life ends, we reach the region of eternal bliss and joy, beyond death and suffering.

We will not add to our karma if we do our daily meditation, develop the ethical virtues, live on a vegetarian diet, avoid alcohol and hallucinogenic or intoxicating drugs, do selfless service, love God and our fellow beings, and attend satsang gatherings. These practices help us from adding to our karma.

Life is about more than attending to our material and physical comfort. There is an aspect of life for which we need to be grateful. Many people live and die without ever exploring their relationship to God. Some saints from the past would say that the difference between the lives of human beings and animals is that humans can know their true spiritual selves.

A man went to heaven, and God told him that he was lucky to have had a human form. The man asked God, "Why are humans special?"

God said, "Peep down upon the earth and you will see what makes humans so special."

God first showed the man the insects.

"See the insects," said God. "Notice that the ants, the worms, and the crawling creatures all have their heads down towards the earth. Even the bees and mosquitoes fly around with their heads looking down."

The man said, "Yes, I can see that."

God said, "Now, look at the reptiles. The snakes and lizards crawl around with their heads facing down to the earth."

Next, God showed the man the birds, saying, "Even

though the birds fly, their heads are always pointing down to the earth. You don't see any birds with their heads flying face up, do you?"

The man said, "You are right. They all fly with their beaks down facing the earth."

God said, "Now look at the mammals. They all crawl around the earth on four legs, with their heads hanging down."

The man said, "So, what makes human beings different?"

God said, "Humans are the only creatures that can look up. They are the only ones that can lift their sights from the world to see God in the spiritual realms above." Human beings have been blessed by God with a special faculty by which we can gain spiritual knowledge. That opportunity is offered to every human being, but few make use of it.

God sends us continual messages hoping to call us back Home. God sends Masters, saints, and mystics to the earth to awaken the desire in humanity to return to their true Home. Some people remain only engaged in taking care of their physical, emotional, and intellectual needs. But some begin to question their existence and the meaning of life and death. When a sincere desire to know the answers awakens, God provides a means to help that soul find the answers.

If we have asked the questions about who we are, if there is God, and what the purpose of life is, we should be grateful to God. If God has put us in touch with a living Master, we can express gratitude. Once we come under the protective wings of a Master, our ultimate emancipation is ensured.

SHOW GRATITUDE BY MAKING
USE OF GOD'S GIFTS

How can we show our gratitude for the miracle of God's love? There are three ways by which we can show gratitude.

One way is to make use of the wonderful gift God has given us. The gift can be of benefit only if put to use. What is the point of receiving a gift and not opening it? Initiation is a gift we do not want to leave on the shelf unopened. By daily meditation, our soul can achieve reunion with God. We are the only species who can know itself as soul and realize it is a part of God. Once initiated, let us make use of that gift by meditating for at least two and a half hours daily. In this way, we can avail of the precious gift given by the Master and steadily travel to our true Home.

The next time the two angels are sent to collect the prayers of human beings, let us not disappoint the one collecting prayers of gratitude. Let us be among those grateful for our gifts. Thank God for our human birth. Thank God for our health. Thank God for our food, clothing, and shelter. Thank God for our families, our education, and our work. Those who have come to a living Master should thank God for leading them to someone who can take them back Home. However, we should not just thank God with our words; we should thank God with our deeds. The deed most appreciated by God is when we put spirituality into practice. We do so by meditating daily. We do so by leading ethical lives of nonviolence, truthfulness, purity, humility, selfless service, and living on a vegetarian diet. We further help ourselves by attending satsang. This way, we differentiate our lives from those of the lesser creatures.

We have in our souls the treasures of all creation. We need to turn within to experience God. We have within us lights more brilliant and wondrous than anything in this physical world. We have uplifting, intoxicating celestial music within more beautiful than the greatest musical performances of this world. The music and harmony of all harmonies within are more enjoyable than listening to any favorite music in the physical world. The inner light and sound radiate rays of love that fill us with more happiness than we could ever dream of. We can enjoy it all year long. The gift of the light and sound is evergreen and ever fresh and keeps us fulfilled forever. The first way to show gratitude to God is to open that gift of light and sound through meditation.

SHOW GRATITUDE TO THE
GIVER BY SERVING GOD'S CREATION

The second way we show gratitude for God's gifts is to share the spirit of divine love with others. We can share our love and light with God's children. We can remove hatred, prejudice, and bigotry from our hearts. We can allow God's creation into our hearts. When we love, we give and share. Let us not turn away from our door anyone in need. Let us consider all as our brothers and sisters, sons and daughters, mothers and fathers.

In the Bible, a talk given by Jesus illustrates the importance of giving and sharing. In this talk, Jesus described that in the future God will come and sit on a throne. God will then separate humanity into two groups of people. He compares the two groups of people as goats and sheep. Jesus describes how God will put the sheep on one side and the goats on the other side.

God will tell the goats that they are being sent away. The goats will ask, "Why?"

God will say, "I was hungry and you gave Me no food. I was thirsty and you gave Me no drink. I was a stranger and you did not welcome Me. I was naked and you did not clothe Me. I was sick and in prison and you did not visit Me."

The goats will be surprised and ask, "When did we see You hungry, thirsty, sick, naked, in prison, or as a stranger, and when did we not take care of You?"

God will tell them, "As you did not serve even the least of your brothers and sisters, you did not serve Me." Then, God will send them away to learn their lesson.

Then God will say to the sheep, "Come, sheep, and inherit My kingdom."

The sheep will ask, "Why do we deserve such a gift?"

God will tell them, "When I was hungry, you gave Me food. When I was thirsty, you gave Me drink. When I was naked, you clothed Me. When I was a stranger, you welcomed Me. When I was sick and in prison, you visited Me."

The sheep will be surprised, and say, "O Lord, when did we see You? When did we feed You, clothe You, give You something to drink, welcome You as a stranger, and visit You in prison or when You were sick?"

The Lord will tell them, "When you have served even the least of your brothers and sisters, you have served Me." Thus, God will bless those sheep with eternal happiness and joy by allowing them to enter God's kingdom.

This teaching parable illustrates a profound truth. It shows the importance God places on sharing with and caring for others.

We know that there is no difference between sheep and goats so far as preferences by God, and that this is a teaching story. We know that God loves all creatures equally. However, by using the analogy of the sheep and goats, Jesus showed the difference between serving others and not serving others. The story illustrates how, though many people say they want to serve God, when asked to help their fellow human beings, they decline and say no. The message pointed out in this story is that in God's eyes, we serve God best when we serve others.

When we develop our spiritual vision, we see the light of God in all. We love all. We see no high and low between people of different religions, faiths, countries, or cultures. We see no high and low between the educated and uneducated. We see no high and low between the rich and the poor. Why? Because when we see God's light in all, we see all as part of one large family of God. Thus, when someone asks us for help, we feel that the God within that person is asking us for help. We, out of love, want to give help to that person.

Selfless service is part of our spiritual development. It has been given two rows on the spiritual introspection diary. One is to note the time we spend in selfless service. The other is to note our failures to serve selflessly. A failure means that we did not help when we could have helped.

Think of how many times someone needs our help. Someone may be hungry, thirsty, poor, or ill, and we may say we are too busy to help. Opportunities to help are many. Let us make use of those opportunities.

We benefit from selfless service, so that when we meditate, we are blessed with greater spiritual upliftment. The spiritual benefit we receive from doing selfless service is equal to the benefit we receive from meditation. We get a boost that fructifies by faster progress in our meditation. Blessed are those that consider all jobs to be work to help God.

When we do seva, we need to make sure it is done selflessly. Selfless service is saying, "Oh, Lord, whatever you want, I am Your servant. You can use my hands to do work for You." Then, we allow ourselves to work without any personal gain for us. If we do so, we will live the real meaning of selfless service.

Gratitude to God translates into acknowledging with humility that our goodness is due to God who created us. Without the Creator, we would not exist.

GRATITUDE THROUGH ACKNOWLEDGING THE DIVINE

The third way we can show gratitude is to acknowledge the existence of the Divine. We may think that there is a separation between science and spirituality, yet even great scientists have acknowledged a divine Creator.

There is an account from the life of Samuel Morse, who was a professor who invented the telegraph. He used to sit in his room at the university doing experiments. He would say that sometimes he would not know what to do next in his experiment. At that time he would pray for more insight. Whenever he did so, an answer would come from within to guide his experiment further. As a result, his invention of the telegraph was successful. Later, whenever he would travel throughout the world and receive praise for his experiments, Dr. Morse would say, "Whenever honors came to me from Europe or America due to the invention of the telegraph I never felt I deserved them." He would say, "I had made a valuable application of electricity, not because I was superior to other men, but solely because God, who meant it for humanity, must reveal it to someone and was pleased to reveal it to me."

It makes sense to us now that when Dr. Samuel Morse sent his first message on the telegraph, it was the following words, "What hath God wrought!" meaning, "What has God brought forth!"

Look at the humility of one who produced one of the great inventions in history. With all the name and fame gained for inventing the telegraph, he knew that this accomplishment was due to the grace of God.

If we measure ourselves against the standards of humility found in many great scientists, how do we fare? We paint a picture, write a song, create a new recipe, build a cabinet, or write a poem, and we think we are great.

If we practiced humility and gratitude, we would give thanks to God for letting us be the instrument of God's accomplishments.

If we are proud of our physical body—our looks, our strength, our stamina, our athletic prowess, our agility, and our good health—let us give thanks to the Lord. Our physical body would not exist if God had not created us.

If we are proud of our mental capabilities and our intellect, our school honors and certificates, our high grades, our education, whether we have been promoted from elementary school or middle school, or have graduated from high school, college, or graduate school, then let us thank the Lord for giving us the gift of intelligence.

If we are proud of our creativity, whether we have created a painting or sculpture, written a song or play, written poetry or books, decorated our home, designed an outfit, or built an architectural wonder, then let us thank God for the gift of creativity. Without God, we would not have the creative mind.

If we have a solvent financial base, with a job or

career, strong assets, good home, and luxuries, let us thank God. We should also thank God for our family and friends.

We should thank God for creating our soul, for without that we would not exist. God has set us into motion by creating parts of God's own self as souls. That is the cause of our whole existence. We may think our existence is our body and mind, but what enlivens those is the soul. If God had not created souls, there would be no life-giving power to enliven the matter that comprises our body and mind. Dissect the body to its smallest components, and we are nothing but a conglomerate mass of atoms bound together into a human being. Dissect the brain, and it is a mass of atoms that form into brain cells. It is all matter. Scientists have now discovered that matter contains within it energy. If atoms are broken down further, they are dancing packets of energy, including waves of light and sound. Scientists have heard the sound coming from atoms. Ultimately, what enlivens matter is spirit. For that, we need to thank God.

Sant Darshan Singh Ji Maharaj put it clearly in this verse:

> *With every breath I must bow to my Friend,*
> *For I owe my life to his grace.*

Every second of our lives is due to the grace of God. Humility means that we recognize that God has created us.

We can show our gratitude by making use of God's gifts by meditating on the inner light and sound, by serving God's creation, and by acknowledging with humility the existence of the Divine, the source of all gifts that enrich our lives.

PERSONAL REFLECTION

List the gifts you have received from God physically, intellectually, emotionally, and spiritually. Spend a week mentally offering God gratitude for these gifts. Note any changes in your daily life and attitude.

12

COMMITMENT TO SPIRITUAL GROWTH

What separates champions and winners from those who do not succeed is commitment. Everyone is born with capabilities and faculties to attain goals. The choices we make separate those who are successful from those who are not.

In the field of sports, some athletes become basketball stars, golf legends, soccer champions, and football heroes. When interviewed about their success, winners focus on the role of their hard work. While others may miss practice, champions stick with whatever it takes to be the best.

Those who excel in medicine, education, technology, or science spend long nights mastering their knowledge.

The principles for success are no different in the spiritual field. The goal of spirituality is union of our soul with God. The method of attaining that is meditation. We can analyze our commitment.

Talking about meditation will not help us. Meditating for five minutes here and there will not get us to our goal. We have "x" number of years in this life. To make the maximum progress in this life, the Masters prescribe a minimum of two and a half hours daily of meditation. If we miss those two and a half hours, do we make it up the next day?

If we are going to school, we get assignments. If we miss an assignment, we can take a lower grade or make it up. Either way, we are responsible to do the work. In spirituality, no one is standing over us with a grade book. Yet, at the end of our life, we will know how far we have advanced. Did we reach our goal of union with God? If not, we still have work to do.

It is true that God has the power to take souls back to the Divine in the blink of an eye. But that is not how the system of creation is set up. There is a system in place where we have to take the steps necessary. God has given us a long rope and about twenty-five percent free will to make choices. Our current life is based on the reactions of past thoughts, words, and deeds for which we must either reap rewards or pay the consequences. Beyond the preordained parts of our lives, affected by our past choices, we have free will.

Those who have merged back in God made the choice to do so. Those people who we know as saints, Masters, teachers, and enlightened beings did whatever was needed. They meditated many hours daily, many while holding a job and raising a family. It is not impossible to do. Where there is a will, there is a way.

Saints talk about the nighttime as a gold mine for spiritual progress. During the day, we have a fixed time that we have to be at work. Our body requires time to bathe, dress, and eat. Our family requires our time and attention. Beyond that, our time is our own. God has given us the night as well as the free hours of the day to engage in meditation.

Kabir Sahib has said in a verse:

Wake up, my loved one: Why do you sleep?
The night is over, why must you also waste your
*   day in slumber?*
Those who are awake attain the jewel.

In this verse, Kabir Sahib is advising us to make the best use of our time in life. If people have the stamina to stay up at night for worldly goals, then that capability is there for us to achieve our spiritual goals. He is also saying that besides using the night for spiritual growth, we should also not slumber through the day. How do we slumber in the day? Although we may engage in our worldly responsibilities and duties, we also slumber by forgetting God during the day. During our waking moments, we can keep God present as we engage in our daily activities, and utilize our spare moments for meditation.

There is a story of a king who was looking for an animal or creature to be his mascot. He did not want just any living creature to have that title. He was king and wanted the best creature to be the mascot representing his kingdom. He asked his ministers to devise a test to see which animal was worthy to be his mascot. The ministers asked the king what criteria were important.

The king thought for a moment and said, "I want a mascot dedicated to attaining a goal and sticking with it."

The ministers met and decided to hold a contest among the animals and creature. The contest would be a race to see which of them could reach the goal line, the gates to the kingdom. In this way, they would see which of them were more dedicated to sticking to the goal of winning the race. Whoever won would be the mascot.

A proclamation was issued to the people saying that each village could select an animal or creature for the competition and line them up at the starting point.

The people thought this was a good chance to earn favor with the king. There were six villages in the kingdom, and each picked the animal they believed would make it to the goal first. They could pick a creature from any species: animal, reptile, amphibian, bird, fish, or insect. The leaders of each village came together to draw straws to see who would pick first, second, third, fourth, fifth, and last.

The members of the first village met and said, "We will win if we pick the lion. After all, the lion is already king of the jungle. There is no question that the lion would win. All the other animals are afraid of the lion. No other animal would dare get in the way of the king of the jungle."

The people in the second village thought, "The lion is already taken, so we have to pick another animal. Let us pick the elephant. This is the strongest and biggest animal in the kingdom. When the elephant runs, all other animals get out of its way so they will not be crushed. The elephant is strong and works hard. This should be the winning mascot."

The citizens of the third village thought the two best choices were already taken. They thought, "Everyone is afraid of the snake. No one will confront the snake. The snake can slither through anything so that it can get ahead when it races to the kingdom's gate." They thought their snake would win.

The members of the fourth village were worried that there were no good choices left. They remembered the story of Aesop's fable in which there was a race between a hare and a tortoise. The villagers forgot that at the end of the story the tortoise beat the hare. Thus, they picked a hare to be in the race.

The people of the fifth village had a really hard time figuring out what to do. They felt that the four best choices were taken. They said, "Well, if we cannot win on strength or speed, we would win on brains. The fox is clever and can figure out a way to win."

The members of the sixth village felt hopeless. They lamented, "All the best animals are taken. There is little chance for us to win." They wracked their brains, trying to figure out whom to pick for their mascot. Luckily for them, they had the wisest person in the kingdom living in their village.

The wise man said, "I have a plan. Let us pick the ant."

The other members of this village said, "An ant? This is the tiniest creature. It will take ages to reach the kingdom. It is so little that anyone can step on it. It is the most vulnerable, the tiniest, and the slowest of all the creatures. It will never make it. Why do you want to pick something that is destined to lose?"

The wise man said, "Don't worry. The ant will

definitely win."

The other villagers thought that maybe he was so wise that he was not practical anymore. With no other viable option since the best animals were already taken, they went along with the wise man and selected the ant to compete.

On the day of the competition, the villagers came out to watch the race. They lined up along the sides of the roadway.

The villagers lined up the lion, the elephant, the snake, the hare, and the fox. The king and his ministers came out to watch. They counted the animals and then announced, "We see the animals from five villages, but we do not see any contestant from the sixth village."

The leader of the sixth village stood up and said, "Our entry is here."

"Where is it?" asked the king's ministers.

The leader of the sixth village said, "It is so tiny you cannot see it well. We have an ant."

The ministers thought the village leader was joking and said, "An ant? Are you kidding? The ant will never win. You must think this is a joke."

The leader said, "No, we are entering the ant and believe it can win."

The starting bell rang out and the race began. All began cheering. They were filled with excitement, each person thinking that their contestant would win.

The lion started out running with a roar. As the lion ran, they thought that it would win. But after running for a short time, the lion saw a deer running on the sidelines. Since he was hungry, he chased down the deer for its dinner. The villagers began screaming for the lion to stop, but the lion ignored them. They thought that surely after eating its dinner the lion would get back on track for the race. However, after eating, the lion yawned, stretched out, and fell asleep.

The other five village members were overjoyed that the lion had succumbed to sleep and thought their animal would have a chance. The second village's members were excited that their elephant was running with good speed. Along the way, the elephant saw a female elephant. Suddenly, the elephant took a left-hand turn off the roadway and went into the forest. For hours and hours they did not see the elephant again.

This gave the other four village members hope. The third village thought the snake would keep slithering down the road towards the kingdom. They felt they had a good chance to win.

Suddenly, the snake saw a mongoose by its snake hole. The snake had hidden some jewels in it and was angered to see the mongoose going down its hole. The snake rushed off the road to its hole. It began hissing in anger at the mongoose. The mongoose held its ground and would not leave, prepared to attack if the snake lunged at it. The snake and mongoose were in a stalemate; neither would leave the snake's hole.

The last three villages were ecstatic that their three worst choices would have a chance.

The leader of the fourth village said, "You see, the hare is the one who will win the race. There is no tortoise so according to the fable it has to win." Suddenly, the hare that had been running along saw some rabbits playing along the side of the road. The hare wanted to play with them and ran off with the other rabbits.

The members of the fourth village began crying out to the hare, "No, get back on the road." However, it was too busy having fun.

The members of the fifth village heaved a sigh of relief. They knew the only competition for their fox was the ant. They said, "The members of the sixth village had picked such a loser to enter the race. We know the clever fox will win."

The members of the fifth village watched their fox run along the road. Suddenly, the fox stopped, having seen a farm where there were chickens sitting on their eggs. The fox had a habit of stealing eggs and stopped to wait for the chickens to leave their eggs.

The members of the sixth village realized that now they had a chance. They were worried when they saw that all of the other five contestants had become distracted with something else. Would their ant also get off track?

The wise man of the sixth village had faith in the ant. How did he know? The night before the race, when everyone in all the villages was sleeping, the wise man had gone out to the road leading from the starting point to the finish line. He took large bottles of water sweetened with sugar. He then laid out a line of sweetened water from the starting point to the kingdom's gates. The next day, when the race was to begin, he placed the ant on the beginning of the trail of sweet water.

Sure enough, the ant followed that line of sugar water. The ant kept going, never stopping for anything.

Despite the cheers and cries of the various villagers to get their contestant moving, none of the other creatures changed their ways. The members of the sixth village were elated and cheered when the lowly ant reached the gates of the kingdom.

The king's ministers were shocked that the lowly ant had won. They wondered what kind of mascot this ant would make.

The king was impressed with the ant's commitment to its goal, but more so by the cleverness of wise man for laying the trail.

"I proclaim the lowly ant as the winner," said the king.

The king and his ministers approached the wise man of the sixth village to ask how he knew to pick the ant.

The wise man said, "Each of these other contestants was waylaid from the goal by a failing of character."

The members of the first village asked, "Why did our lion lose? Isn't the lion the king of the jungle?"

The wise man explained, "The lion may be declared king of the jungle, and others fear it, but it lost because it is full of ego. It knows that it can have any animal it wants for its food. The lion knows that there is no need for it to stay on a task. It can take rest and slumber whenever it wants. Whenever it is ready to eat, it can stalk another animal. Thus, it knows that all are at its beck and call, and it does not have to work hard. It is so full of itself that there is no need for it to compete. The lion does not care to do anything to better itself. Goals do not mean anything, as it can get what it wants whenever it wants. Its ego keeps it from achieving anything other than what it wants at the moment."

The second group of villagers said, "We do not understand why the elephant lost."

The wise man explained, "The elephant is known for its lust. It was so focused on the female elephant that it lost sight of the goal. It got so entangled with satisfying its lust that it lost track of the goal."

The third group of villagers asked, "Then why did the snake lose?"

The wise man explained, "The snake is filled with anger. Any time it does not get its way it hisses and bites— it has no control over its anger. It was so angry that the mongoose would come near its hole that it could not focus on the race. It gets so caught up in anger and revenge that it cannot think of anything else. That is why the snake lost focus and lost the race."

The fourth group of villagers said, "The hare is supposed to be a fast animal. Since there was no tortoise in the race, it should have won. Why did it lose?"

The wise man said, "The hare is filled with attachment for the other rabbits. Once it gets caught up in playing with them and being with them that is all that matters to it. It enjoys being with those it loves. It is so attached to them that it cannot focus on its goal."

The fifth group finally asked, "What about the fox? It is supposed to be clever. Why did it lose?"

The wise man said, "Did you notice what the fox did? It was so intent upon looking for a chance to steal the chicken's eggs that it left the race. The fox is filled with greed. It is not content with its own share of what it gets, but wants what others have. It is greedy and wants to take what belongs to others. It does not live by its own hard work, but wants to take from others. That is what caused it to leave the race and stay focused on stealing."

All the other villagers then said, "We understand what has happened to the creature we selected for the race, but how did this insignificant ant win?"

The wise man said, "An ant is a hard worker and is diligent. Once it sets itself on a task, it stays with it until it is done. Also, the ant is dedicated to following a trail. Once a path is laid out for the ant, it follows it diligently. It does not get distracted. It does not step off the trail to engage in other activities. The ant stays on the trail until it reaches the trail's end. It also enjoys sweets and savors the taste of sweet water. The more sweet water it has, the more sweet water it wants. Each time the ant tasted the water on the trail, it wanted more. This is what drove the ant to the finish line."

The king was pleased with the wise man's explanation and happily named the ant as the winner.

This story illustrates aspects of the human condition. If we ask every human being, "Do you want to find God?" they will most likely answer, "Yes." But if you lay out the path by which they can find God, only a few will reach the gates of the Lord. People will go off track for the same reasons that the creatures in the story went off track. Ego, lust, anger, attachment, and greed will throw human beings off the track.

These are called the five thieves that keep us from God. The mind uses these thieves as a way to keep us from reaching the end goal of the gates of the kingdom of God.

Like ego waylaid the lion in the story, ego keeps us focused on ourselves instead of God. When our ego is in its full glory, it makes us think we do not need God. It tells us that we are all-knowing. It blocks us from looking for a teacher who can lead us to God. It tells us that we are already perfect and that God will open the gates when we leave this world, without us doing anything. Like the lion, we think we are already the king of our own jungle, and that God is going to embrace us without us doing any spiritual work. We spend our lives in a slumber. We consider all others to be inferior to us and place them at our beck and call to take care of all our needs. We may lord over them in the workplace, at home, or in society. We expect our friends, community, and society to cater to us. We think we are number one, and everyone else should be subservient to us. We think God is there to serve us.

Lust distracted the elephant. In the same way, lust is another thief that keeps us away from God. It is one thing to love others in this world, but in lust, we forget God and focus on fulfilling our own desires. Lust can be for sensual pleasures, alcohol, drugs, gambling, or any habit that distracts our focus from the goal of returning to God.

The snake was taken off track by anger. It was so focused on its own anger that it forgot its purpose. If we reflect on our lives, we can see how we become entangled in anger. How many things make us angry? We get angry with anyone who does not fulfill our expectations of him or her. Sometimes we cannot contain our anger, and we want to take revenge. We start planning what we want to do to the person who made us angry. The anger occupies our thoughts, words, and deeds, and we lose track of our spiritual goal.

The hare was distracted by its attachment to the other hares. It felt that playing with the other rabbits was more important than anything else was. In the same way, people put everyone else but God first in their lives and do not make it to the goal.

The fox was taken off course by its greed. There are people who are never content with what they have but want more. They spend all their waking time trying to accumulate more, instead of balancing their lives with finding the Lord. Some people accumulate possessions. Some want to increase their power, name, or fame. Greed drives people to be like the fox who wanted to steal. In this way, they lose sight of spending time in returning to God.

Those who end up like the five creatures in the story

have been sidetracked from their goal. The condition of these people can be described by this verse of Kabir:

> *You have wasted your life in sleep and the day*
> *is passed in feeding the body;*
> *Alas! The invaluable jewel of life has been*
> *cheaply traded away.*

Each of the creatures in the story traded away the attainment of a kingly goal for the desires of their physical existence. They could have had the admiration of the king. Instead, the lion got his food, the elephant got fulfillment of desires, the snake got the small little snake hole, the hare got to play with the other rabbits, and the fox got the chicken eggs. It was only the ant that won the king's approval.

Similarly, we can enter the kingdom of God, but we are trading away that jewel of life for sleeping, eating, and taking care of our desires.

If we want to return to God, we can take a lesson from the ant. Once the ant started on the track, it followed it to the end. It did not waver, but kept focused on one thing—following the trail. It did not stop to consider, "Oh, I am not there yet, so let me give up." It kept going one step at a time, putting in the effort until it reached its goal.

Besides effort, there was another factor that caused the ant to succeed. Its quality of sticking to its goal attracted the help of the wise man. He laid out its track. This is what a spiritual Master does for us. Whenever we have the desire to reach the goal of finding God, a Master intervenes by putting us on the right track. He makes sure we do not take a wrong turn.

A spiritual Master lays out the steps for us to reach God. If we move along the track, without deviating from the course, we will reach our goal. Step one is receiving initiation into the light and sound of God. For this, the only requirements are to be vegetarian, avoid alcohol and hallucinogenic, intoxicating, and recreational drugs, and to earn one's livelihood honestly. Step two is that once initiated, we meditate on the light and sound daily for a minimum of two and a half hours. Step three is that we keep an introspection diary of our thoughts, words, and deeds to weed out the mind's attempt to engage us in anger, lust, greed, attachment, and ego by developing nonviolence, truthfulness, purity, humility, and selfless service. Step four is that we focus on God. For that we receive upliftment by going to satsang where we hear instructive teachings in a spiritually-charged atmosphere. Step five is that we perform selfless service. This is the track laid out for us.

The Master also does more for us besides laying out the track. In the story, the wise man did not just lay out a track for the ant; knowing that ants like sugar and water, he also put a trail of sweet water along the track. This is what a Master does for us. He lays along our track the sweet water of Shabd or Naam—the current of light and sound—the nectar of God. A Master initiates us into the light and sound—the sweet water—of God.

The light and sound are not physical phenomena like outer sunlight and sounds of this world. The inner light and sound current is a vibration made of God's essence. We know how we feel love when we are around certain people. Nothing can be seen happening with the outer eyes, but there is a vibration of energy passing between the two people. This is a small reflection of what happens when soul comes in contact with God. God is an ocean of consciousness. Our soul is of the same essence. When we withdraw our attention from the mind and body, we are conscious of our true self as soul. While attached to the mind and body, we are not aware of our soul.

After experiencing the light and sound current, and the bliss it brings, we want more. The arc of our effort in the form of our steps and the grace in the form of the Master laying more bliss continue, until one day we will find ourselves in the kingdom of God.

The sugar of Naam fulfills us. The more we taste that sugar through meditation, the less attracted we are to the worldly distractions.

When filled with the delicious taste of the sugar of God's love, we lose our ego. We become immersed in that sugar of love, wanting only to drink its sweetness.

When filled with the delicious taste of the sugar of God's love, we are no longer distracted by lust. The love of God is more fulfilling and satisfying than any loves of this world. While the loves of this world can make us happy, the love of God's embrace permeates every pore of our being through our soul.

When filled with the sugar of God's love, we are no longer distracted by situations that make us angry. We are so intoxicated with God's love that we do not get angry at what others are doing.

When filled with the sugar of God's love, we are no longer distracted by attachment. We fulfill our duties with love, but our attention remains on God. In our hearts we love God all the time, even when we serve our family, friends, and society.

When filled with the sugar of God's love, we are not distracted by greed. We find that nothing of this world is as satisfying as God's love. We work hard to earn a living, and we are content with what we have. We use what we have to support our family and ourselves. We find that there is no computer activity as fulfilling as time spent absorbed in the ecstasy of connecting with God. We are grateful for what we receive from God.

All those committed to their spiritual goals are like the ant. Whether billionaires, famous artists, inventors, or anyone who tops their field, they share the common quality of commitment to a goal. They work without stopping until their goal is reached. If it takes working throughout the night, they do so. Saints have made use of every spare moment to meditate on God. If we commit to the goal of meditation, we can reach union of our soul with God.

Initiation alleviates our greatest fears: aging and death. Saints come with a consistent message that we are not the body; rather, we are an immortal soul. We are spirit, an eternal spark. To know our true self, we can invert our attention to discover this hidden essence.

There is an interesting story about a river. The river's

journey began at the top of a mountain. It flowed down the mountain, passing the trees along the shore. It skipped over rocks and sometimes dipped into little waterfalls on its travel. Suddenly, the river met a desert and did not know what to do. It was used to flowing along a riverbed, but now the riverbed was coming to an end and there was nothing but dry sand for miles and miles.

The river said, "I am used to crossing anything that comes in my path, so I will flow across the sand." The river tried to cross the sand, but every time it set foot on the sand, its waters dried up. It would be absorbed into the sand and disappear.

"This is strange," said the river. "This never happened to me before. How am I going to cross this desert?"

Suddenly, the sands of the desert spoke to the river and said, "The winds cross the sand."

The river said, "That is true. The wind flies across the sand."

The sand advised the river, "You must not try to cross the sand yourself for your water droplets will sink into the sand and you will be drained of all your water. You must let the wind carry you across or your entire waters will disappear into the sand."

The stream was perplexed and wondered, "How can the wind carry me across?"

The sand explained, "Watch the wind. It carries things across me all the time. It can lift up the water within you and carry it across the desert. Then, it will drop you off on the other side."

The river said, "I am such a long river, with countless drops of water. How can the wind, made of light air, carry my heavy water droplets?"

The sand said, "The wind has done that for water before, and can do it for you also. Trust us. You must try it for yourself to prove it. If you don't let the wind take you, your water will stop here, and you will slowly disappear as you get soaked into the sand."

The river complained, "Can you guarantee the truth of what you are telling me?"

The sand said, "If you don't try it, you will surely die. Your water will be soaked into us, and there will be nothing left of you. There is no harm in asking the wind to take you across."

The river then requested the wind to help it cross the desert so it would not disappear and die.

The river asked, "How can you do this, though? I am so much heavier than you."

The wind said, "You do not understand your true nature. If you did, you would know that the wind could carry you. If you knew what your true nature was, you would happily rise up and fly with me."

The river contemplated its true nature, and realized that at its core, it too was made of the gases oxygen and hydrogen. Its true essence was vapor. As soon as it realized its true essence, the water droplets rose up as vapor and flew into the arms of the wind.

The wind carried the river's drops as vapor across the desert for many miles. The river was in ecstasy as it flew above the earth in the embrace of the wind. Then, when the wind reached the end of the desert, there was a mountain.

As the vapor cooled, it turned back into water and fell as rain. The rain accumulated and flowed down the mountainside, forming a new river. The river continued to flow until it reached the sea and became one with it.

This tale describes the human condition. We are like the river. A day will come when we will meet the desert and dry up. Our end will come. If we think we are the body, we will be in fear, just as the river feared drying up in the sands of the desert. There is a mighty wind that can carry us across to the other side. A Master connects us with the mighty wind that lifts us across the sands of time. That mighty wind is a current known as the light and sound of God.

This light and sound current passes through all realms of creation. The soul within us is spirit, a spark of the Divine. If we can uplift that spark to connect with the light and sound, we can travel on it back to its Source. The river water realized that its true nature was the invisible vapor and that in this form it could fly; similarly, we realize our true nature is the soul that can soar back to God. When we identify with our soul, we too can spread our wings to fly into the higher spiritual realms beyond this physical world. We can cross the threshold of death and realize the realms of immortality.

As the water had to become its true nature of vapor in order to fly, so must we shed our outer illusion of the body to become our true nature of the soul in order to fly into the immortal realms of spirit. The river could return to its true source, the sea, just as we can return to our true Source, the eternal sea of consciousness, called God.

The wind helped the water travel to its source. Similarly, the Masters connect us with the spiritual current of light and sound that can help us reach God. The Masters come to lift us up and carry us in their arms back to our original Source. All we need to do is try the experiment of going within to find our true self as soul. By going within, we find we are not the face that looks back at us from a mirror. We are an effulgent, radiant soul, full of light. When we realize our self, then we can fly over the sands of life, and be restored to the ocean of love from where we came.

The sand told the river to prove the truth of the power of the wind for itself before it would believe. We too can try the experiment of going within through meditation on the light and sound to experience the proof that our true self is the soul, a part of God, and that there is something beyond this physical world. The risk of not trying it is that the days of our lives will run out, and we will face the end of our body. Do we want to meet our end not knowing what awaits us in the beyond, or do we want to meet our last days in full knowledge of the beyond? Unless we discover our true nature during our lifetime, we will live in fear of the unknown. We will be shaken by the fear of death. However, if we meditate, we will witness the glory and grandeur of the inner realms. We will travel to the Ocean from where our soul came, the immortal land of God.

To meditate, we do not need to change our religion. It is not a process of conversion; rather it is a process of inversion. It is a nondenominational form of meditation that can be integrated with one's own religion, faith, and culture. We merely sit in a comfortable position, close our eyes gently as we do when we go to sleep, and gaze into the middle of what we see lying in front of us. In the introductory form of meditation, which one can practice before being initiated in the light and sound by a spiritual Master, we can mentally repeat any name of God with which we feel comfortable. At the time of initiation, one learns the full meditation instructions for the Shabd meditation, which consists of two practices: meditation on the inner light (simran practice) and meditation on the inner sound (bhajan practice.)

For the meditation on the inner light or simran practice, a spiritual Master gives five charged Words to repeat mentally to keep the mind still. These Words keep the mind occupied so that no thoughts can distract our gaze from focusing within.

Through repetition of these five Words, charged by a spiritual Master, our attention focuses at the third or single eye, between and behind the two eyebrows. From there, it starts to experience light. It may see flashes of light, circles of light, or lights of any color, such as golden, white, yellow, orange, blue, violet, green, or purple. By focusing into the middle of the light, we become absorbed. We may see an inner sky, stars, a moon, and a sun. Then, the radiant or ethereal form of the spiritual Master appears and takes us on an inner journey.

At the time of initiation we also learn the second

practice, which is meditation on the inner sound. In this practice, we listen to the celestial melody, which is reverberating ceaselessly within us. This enchanting melody magnetizes the soul and uplifts it into the spiritual realms beyond.

Wondrous regions lie beyond this physical realm. Descriptions of these mystic lands have been given by saints. As one ascends to higher regions, one experiences greater consciousness. While on the earth, we are part of the physical region, consisting of mostly matter. Thus, we have the least amount of consciousness. The greatest light we know in this region is that of the stars and sun, and this is but a dim light compared to the light in the highest regions. What we experience as the greatest love on earth is a dim reflection of the love we experience as we soar into higher realms. Those who met the being of light at the threshold of death said that it emanated a love greater than they had ever received from any love of this world. The light is greater than any light they experienced on earth. If the love and light at the threshold of death and at the beginning of the higher regions are so great, think how much greater is the light and love in still higher regions. It is a light that is soothing and all embracing.

Each region is filled with divine music. The energy emanating from God is a principle that manifests as light and sound. The sound is a divine melody that reverberates without instruments or vocal chords. It is a vibratory sound that emits various sounds in each region. The sound changes along with the vibratory rate of the degree of consciousness or the amounts of spirit and matter in each region. The more matter, the less ethereal the sound. The more consciousness, the more ethereal the sound.

In the higher regions we are free from the cycle of the lower worlds and out of the realms of karma. Those who enter here have learned God's law of the universe— the law of love. Every breath is permeated with love; they are imbued with love. Thus, they have no thoughts, words, or deeds that consist of anything but God's love. They are the enlightened souls who we know to be the embodiments of love. We all know of examples of numerous saints and mystics who have graced this world. Masters, saints, mystics, and founders of all religions have visited the spiritual regions beyond and taught the people of their times to do the same. A living spiritual Master comes to give us a connection to the spark of the Divine, leading to spiritual consciousness.

Let us fly on the winds of the divine current of light and sound. All we have to do is learn how to meditate on that light and sound so that our soul can rise into the wondrous realms. Meditation enables us to make our connection with the spark of the Divine and reunite our individual fire with the Eternal Flame of the Divine.

PERSONAL REFLECTION

Reflect on what you want to achieve spiritually. Make an action plan. List the steps you can take to reach that goal and outline how you can commit to making your plan a reality.

ABOUT THE AUTHOR

Sant Rajinder Singh Ji Maharaj is an internationally-recognized spiritual Master of meditation on the inner light and sound, president of the Human Unity Conference, and head of Science of Spirituality, a nonprofit, nondenominational organization that provides a forum for people to learn meditation, experience personal transformation, and bring about inner and outer peace and human unity.

He has presented his powerful, yet simple meditation on the inner light and sound to millions of people throughout the world through seminars, meditation retreats, television and radio shows and Internet broadcasts, magazines, and books.

His method of achieving inner and outer peace through meditation has been recognized by civic, religious, and spiritual leaders. He convened the 16th International Human Unity Conference in Delhi, India; was president of the 7th World Religions Conference; was a major presenter at the Parliament of the World Religions held in Chicago in 1993 and the World Conference on Religion and Peace held in Rome and Riva del Garde, Italy, in 1994. He hosts annual international conferences on Human Integration and Global Mysticism. At the 50th Anniversary of the United Nations celebration held at the Cathedral of St. John the Divine, Sant Rajinder Singh opened the program by putting thousands of people into meditation. He has received numerous awards, tributes, and honorary welcomes from civic and religious heads around the world.

He is a best-selling author whose many books include, *Inner and Outer Peace through Meditation, Empowering Your Soul*

through Meditation, *Silken Thread of the Divine*, *Spiritual Pearls for Enlightened Living*, *Spiritual Thirst*, *Visions of Spiritual Unity and Peace*, *Ecology of the Soul*, *Education for a Peaceful World*, and many books in Hindi, including *Spirituality in Modern Times* and *True Happiness*. His publications have been translated into fifty languages. He also has many CDs, DVDs, and hundreds of articles published in magazines, newspapers, and journals throughout the world. He has appeared on television, radio, and Internet broadcasts worldwide. Sant Rajinder Singh holds meditation seminars and gives public lectures throughout North America, South America, Europe, Africa, Asia, Australia, and Oceania. He can be contacted at the Science of Spirituality Center, 4 S. 175 Naperville Rd., Naperville, IL 60563; Tele: (630) 955-1200; FAX: (630) 955-1205 or at Kirpal Ashram, Sant Kirpal Singh Marg, Vijay Nagar, Delhi, India 110009; Tele: 91-11-2-7117100; FAX: 91-11-2-7214040; or visit www.sos.org